**Teaching and Learning
through the National Curriculum**

Series Editor Roger Trend

Teaching Geography at Key Stage 2

Bill Chambers and Karl Donert
Liverpool Hope University College

Chris Kington Publishing
CAMBRIDGE

© Bill Chambers and Karl Donert
ISBN 1 899857 27 3

First published 1996 by
Chris Kington Publishing
27 Rathmore Road
Cambridge CB1 4AB
Reprinted 1997

Dedication
The authors wish to dedicate this book to a long French summer and to Nicole, Fiona, William, Anastasia, Gregory and Clair.

British Library Cataloguing in Publication Data. A catalogue record for this book is available from the British Library.

Design by Barry Perks Graphic Design
Printed in the United Kingdom by York Publishing Services Ltd, 64 Hallfield Road, Layerthorpe, York YO3 7XQ

Contents

Series Statement

Teaching and Learning through the National Curriculum is a series of books for teachers, student teachers and others involved in the education of children aged 3 to 15 years. Each book has a main subject focus and is concerned with a single key stage (1, 2 or 3). It provides stimulus and insight for experienced teachers and sound practical advice for those new to the profession. Each is based on three main themes: key issues, the National Curriculum and information technology.

The first chapter provides an up to date analysis of educational matters which often goes beyond the immediate concerns of the National Curriculum. Each author identifies the key issues which warrant systematic attention and which take the reader into some of the important educational issues of the 1990s. The issues vary between subjects and key stages but all reflect what is considered important by the authors who are accomplished practitioners in their respective fields.

The second chapter focuses on National Curriculum matters and each author provides a rationale for a range of teaching strategies appropriate to the subject and key stage. Examples are used to illustrate particular ideas and these are supported by copyright waived pages for teachers to use in the classroom or for INSET. The main function of this chapter is to provide teachers with examples and illustrations of classroom practice.

The third chapter in each book provides the reader with guidance on information technology for the appropriate subject and key stage. This series aims to bridge the gulf between rhetoric and reality by showing how the teaching and learning of that subject can be enhanced through accessible IT materials.

This series will make an effective contribution to subject-focused teaching and learning at Key Stages 1, 2 and 3. As a series, it provides an authoritative and up to date discussion of the 1995 National Curriculum and sets the issues in a broader framework of teaching and learning.

References and Bibliography are given for further reading.

Foreword

Bill Chambers and Karl Donert are well known by teachers as authors in the field of geography education. They have written a book which is totally up to date in its coverage of current issues and thoroughly grounded in their own professional experiences. The entire book is closely tied to National Curriculum requirements, but the first chapter goes well beyond these. The Key Issues selected by the authors for special consideration are diverse and include OFSTED, special educational needs, fieldwork, resources and using adults other than teachers. The National Curriculum is more closely targeted in the second chapter, where matters are addressed through critical analysis. Practical examples and illustrations are used throughout, providing readers with ample stimulus.

The chapter on information technology is particularly significant and will be of interest to all teachers and student teachers who are seeking to develop children's understanding of geographical matters through IT.

The book reflects the extensive experience of both authors in initial and in-service teacher education and in academic geography. Such expertise is brought to bear most effectively through a series of discussions and well illustrated analyses of issues which will be of direct interest to Key Stage 2 teachers.

Roger Trend
Assistant Director (Initial Professional Studies)
School of Education
University of Exeter

Acknowledgements

The following are gratefully acknowledged:

Andy English for drawings: *Figures 1.2, 1.3, 3.3*
Terry Moore for the photograph: *Figure 3.5*
The Met Office, Bracknell for Met FAX: *Figure 3.7*
Firthwood Primary School, Northwood, Middlesex for the home page: *Figure 3.15*

Chapter 1: Key Issues

Key Issue 1: The Pivotal Role of OFSTED

Teaching and learning geography at Key Stage 2 can be one of the most rewarding activities for teachers and pupils alike. The resources now available in schools include highly stimulating videos and magnificent posters and photographs. All participants can relate their own experiences in travel (from local to global) and can identify, for example, with people at risk from natural hazards. Furthermore, the subject lends itself very easily to a wide range of learning activities. The effective teacher exploits these features of the subject and enhances learning by providing children with experiences which foster an inquisitive attitude. An additional bonus is that such work impresses the OFSTED inspectors!

There are many other issues which influence the Key Stage 2 teacher and which relate directly to the work of the Office for Standards in Education (OFSTED). This first Key Issue deals with those which impinge directly on the teaching of geography.

In its annual reviews of inspection findings, OFSTED has consistently identified a number of areas which would benefit from closer attention in primary schools. These include:

1. The problem of topic work.
2. The need for INSET (in-service education and training).
3. The need for geography coordination and management.

Specific to Key Stage 2 were concerns about "the better showing at Key Stage 1 overall" (OFSTED, 1993) compared with Key Stage 2. They commented on the "pattern of weaker performance at Key Stage 2" (OFSTED, 1995) and the fact that schools had found it "difficult to interpret the geography Order, to create a manageable curriculum which focuses on the requirements of the programmes of study". In general, "the practices of assessment, recording and reporting caused difficulties" (OFSTED, 1995).

OFSTED and Topic Work

The problem of topic work in primary schools, identified long ago in *The Teaching and Learning of History and Geography in the Primary School* (HMI, 1989), remains with us in the 1990s:

standards of work in geography often suffered when the subject was taught as part of a broad topic which attempted to integrate aspects of several subjects under a common theme. In these cases geography was marginal or incidental to the main thrust of the topic and, as a result, the treatment was superficial (OFSTED, 1993).

Two years later OFSTED again commented that:

within topic work especially at Key Stage 2, schools need to plan and focus more sharply on the geographical objectives of the work (OFSTED, 1995).

What are the causes of this problem?

In primary schools there are full teaching timetables, demands from all sides to broaden the curriculum, the dominance of the core subjects of mathematics, English, science and design and technology, and a predominance of teachers initially trained in English, history and other arts-orientated subjects. Attempts have been made to use topic work as a pot-pourri of subjects which satisfies few, except perhaps headteachers who seek one simple solution to the need to teach many subjects and to foster children's acquisition of the key generic skills (ie speaking and listening, reading and writing, using and applying mathematics, handling data and experimental and investigative science). When, in addition, the notion of 'geography as a body of knowledge' is replaced by the notion of 'geography as an approach to the study of place', it is no surprise that the subject becomes subsumed under the guise of broad and wide ranging topics in which clear subject-specific geographical objectives are rarely met. Clearly, all topics need to be assessed against their geographical objectives before they can satisfactorily be accepted as geographical (see Supplementary Materials 1).

Subject-based or Broad-based Topics?

The School Curriculum and Assessment Authority (SCAA) recognises the need for subject-based units rather than broad-based topics: "units of work will draw, in the first instance, on work from a single subject or aspect of the curriculum" (SCAA, 1995). The authors also state that "once a manageable framework of ...work has been established" curriculum coherence can be strengthened by "linking together, where appropriate, units of work from different subjects or aspects of the curriculum."

Figure 1.1 shows examples from geography quoted by SCAA which link, on the one hand, weather and rivers with science and, on the other hand, grid references with mathematics. At a more complex level geography, with art

and science, contributes to a topic on *Clothes*; with history to a topic on *Our Local Area*; with Science to *Our Changing Water Supply*; and with mathematics and information technology to *More Fast Food?* (SCAA, 1995).

The Need for INSET and Geography Coordination and Management

Geography is not a core subject in the National Curriculum. It is perceived as being of minor importance by some teachers, and others, with no immediate commitment to the subject. It is, therefore, not surprising to read that "a

Topic Title		Links with Other Subjects
Contrasts in Settlement **Single Subject** Year 5 or 6	Similarities and differences between settlements in different parts of the world Villages, towns and cities in UK, Netherlands and India Children will: Use atlas and maps to locate places Use photos, weather data, CD-ROMS, to compare physical and human features Draw maps of land use in each locality, and links with neighbouring settlements Use newspaper and TV reports to investigate a land use issue.	Geography only
Time	**Geography: 20 Hours**	
Our Changing Water Supply **Two Subjects** Year 5 or 6	Use and management of water locally Link with weather, rivers, environmental change and school locality Link with water cycle, properties of water and microorganisms	Geography and Science
	Children will: Find out about water in the locality (rain, rivers) related to the water cycle	Geography and Science
	Consider water flow Investigate evaporation and condensation	Science
	Water use and local water supply Proposals for a new reservoir and its impact Water demand nationally and overseas	Geography
	Water quality and combatting river pollution	Science
Time	**Geography: 20 Hours Science: 6 hours**	
More Fast Food? **Three Subjects** Year 5 or 6	Consider proposal to set up fast food restaurant in local shopping precinct	Geography Maths IT
	Children will: Explore background to proposal	Geography
	Design questionnaire and computer database to explore local opinion and collect data Make decisions about how to present and interpret data and draw preliminary conclusions Prepare a report with recommendations to the local Planning Office	Geography Maths IT
	Consider national trends in growth of fast food outlets Referring to national statistics and trends, calculate average trends and implications for urban life	Geography Maths
Time	**Geography: 7 Hours Maths: 7 hours IT: 2 hours**	

Figure 1.1 Linking geography with science, IT and mathematics. Source: Schools Curriculum and Assessment Authority (1995) Planning the Curriculum at Key Stages 1 and 2. London, SCAA.

major INSET investment is required to improve teachers' geographical competencies particularly in Key Stage 2", and that, for geography at Key Stages 1 and 2, "the management and organisation of the subject were inadequate in three-quarters of schools" (OFSTED, 1995).

OFSTED and The Need for INSET

Given the low priority attached by many schools and individual teachers to geography, the situation described in the quotation above is likely to continue into the foreseeable future, until the core subjects and the other foundation subjects are well embedded into the whole school curriculum. In such a circumstance it is likely that the coordinator for geography (or humanities) will have a supreme and isolated responsibility for the subject. Notwithstanding this, it should be noted that even if the subject is of low priority within the profession as a whole, the level of teacher interest in geographical topics is often high, both in terms of personal interest and professional competence (see Figure 1.2). In particular:

1. Many teachers are travellers.
2. Many are members of environmental and heritage movements.
3. Many are attracted by rivers.
4. All are interested in the weather.
5. Many visit towns and villages as part of their own recreation.
6. Most need, use and even draw maps.
7. Professionally, many teachers are aware that geography provides a meaningful context in which to do their pictograms and histograms (eg traffic census).
8. Many recognise that geographical data collection, analysis and display provide many opportunities for the use of IT.
9. All are aware that fieldwork appeals to a wide range of pupils.
10. All see that fieldwork can lead to success for pupils who otherwise might not gain such success in other curriculum areas.
11. Many appreciate that fieldwork provides insight into the personalities of children (and colleagues!).
12. All see that geography provides opportunities for many different and contrasting approaches to learning.

Additionally, geography remains one of the most popular subjects at GCSE and GCE Advanced Level, so basic

Figure 1.2 The teacher and geography.

geographical competence and interest among primary teachers may be higher than is often assumed.

National provision of INSET for teaching geography is unlikely to extend beyond GEST (Grants for Education Support and Training) coordinator training and its associated cascade into the whole school through example or school-based INSET. Even the GEST provision is currently under threat and twenty-day courses have been reduced to ten- and even seven- or five-day courses. Local authority support has disappeared in many districts. Similarly, within the school the allocation of time for geography at 'Baker Day' or twilight sessions is likely to be limited, given competing demands.

OFSTED and The Subject Coordinator

The pessimistic scenario described above means that the role of the subject coordinator becomes even more crucial, both informally and formally. This again demands much of the typical coordinator, acting in his/her role as class teacher, coordinator for more than one curriculum and (for geography) probably a newly qualified teacher (NQT).

As Morgan (1991) feared:

Due to the designation of geography as a foundation subject in the National Curriculum and its arrival on stream following the three core subjects and technology, many schools are appointing relatively inexperienced teachers to take charge of not only geography, but often history and RE as well. Alternatively it may be the head or deputy who picks it up after other responsibilities have been allocated. It is likely that in many cases, and for whatever reasons, post holders will be in need of considerable support.

At the very least the coordinator will be expected to:

1. Design, manage and evaluate the curriculum and its associated documentation.
2. Manage the resources.
3. Facilitate staff development.

All of this requires the support of the headteacher and, to a slightly lesser extent, other school staff. Headteachers (and governors) will need to be convinced of the importance of specialist equipment, resources and timetable time, including that needed for fieldwork. As an aside, it is often assumed that OFSTED's regular inspections will ensure the provision of a documented geography policy eventually, but implementation is another thing! On the whole, class teachers will require confidence building and the provision of up to date curriculum information, together with resources which are purchased, managed and accessed in a clear and simple way. It is vital that any lack of knowledge or self-confidence on the part of colleagues is not under-estimated, given the requirement for most primary teachers to be experts in so many aspects of the curriculum.

Key Issue 2: The Role of Geography at Key Stage 2

Some Areas for Concern

There is little doubt that, beyond the world of geographers and the Geographical Association, the role seen for geography is limited, as outlined in the following four points.

First, despite its many weaknesses and complexities (Ranger, 1995) the original and subsequent versions of the geography National Curriculum never attracted the same level of public criticism or debate as that associated with history and English.

Second, it has been argued that, but for the best efforts of the Geographical Association, geography would have been marginalised within the National Curriculum. In particular, the GA ensured "vigorous organisation, promoting the subject in schools and providing INSET opportunities, not least by its publications such as *Teaching Geography* and the increasingly effective *Primary Geographer*" (OFSTED, 1995). The case for geography was further strengthened through other GA publications such as *A Case for Geography* (Bailey and Binns, 1987) and *Geography in the National Curriculum* (Daugherty, 1989). There was also a series of proactive initiatives which included the 1988 meeting of the Association with the then Secretary of State for Education, Sir Keith Joseph. It is pertinent to note that such marginalisation is precisely what has subsequently happened to the subject at Key Stage 4 where it is now optional (Dearing, 1994).

Third, anecdotal evidence from GEST 20-day geography courses indicates the slow (or non-existent) purchasing of geography resources (confirmed by OFSTED, 1995).

Last, evidence also indicates that the allocation of newly trained and often non-specialist teachers to geography coordinator roles is part of a continuing marginalisation of the subject.

Clearly, if geography is to survive the next National Curriculum review at the millennium, teachers and others will have to make a strong case in the face of competition where "the need for science and technology and for language skills will be still more evident" (Blyth and Krause, 1995).

The Strengths of Geography as a Curriculum Subject

Geography offers much to enrich the education of 4 to 11 year olds, as identified in the following six paragraphs.

First, everything that happens in the world occurs in a spatial context. The first question on hearing news, for many people, is "where did it occur?". As children mature they become increasingly aware that each place is different from all others, although as they get even older they also appreciate that places have basic and recurrent similarities. There are fundamental similarities between places, whilst accepting that the weather in Lima is drier than it is in Liverpool, the Andes are higher and steeper than the

Models can help children with their understanding of spatial relationships and local features.

Pennines and the River Maranon is larger than the Mersey. Similarly, the village of Tambogrande has fewer services than Woolton village and the environmental change associated with deforestation of the Amazon forest is progressing faster than the school-based tree planting in the Mersey Forest.

Second, all children have their own 'little geographies', whether it be Carmen de la Legua in Lima or the Edge Hill district of Liverpool. All live in a communal context in which most people are trying to improve their lot, yet all live in an interdependent world where the economic, political and environmental decisions made by international companies and governments ultimately have an impact on their environmental and economic situation.

Third, geography provides a context and a view of the whole world which can lead children to an understanding of local and global issues, including:

1. Relations between Less Economically-Developing Countries (LEDCs) and More Economically-Developing Countries (MEDCs).
2. Immigration.
3. Trade and aid.
4. Development and conservation.
5. Pollution and improvement.
6. Action for the environment.

Geography is concerned with the physical environment, including climate and weather, landscape and landforms, and the way in which the natural environment influences, interacts with and is managed by human and other biological agencies.

Fourth, although knowledge of the location of people, places and events (sometimes called disparagingly "capes and bays geography") is only one small and dated facet of geography, it remains important, as evidenced by the inclusion of maps A, B and C in the Key Stage 2 geography Order (Supplementary Materials 2). Locational knowledge provides the hanger on which the subject is hung and on which concepts can be built. Without such locational knowledge no child can develop a mental map on which to hang the day to day events of life which consequently become a succession of unrelated 'out theres'.

Fifth, geography also includes a range of skills and methodologies. The enquiry approach, in no way unique to geography, is enhanced by the study of geographical issues and topics, whilst the use of geographical skills such as map work and graphicacy make important contributions to learning far beyond the geography lesson. Fundamental to geography is the study of the real world at first hand, through fieldwork. Places beyond the classroom provide a geographer's laboratory in which children can be taught how to observe, record and explain the forms and processes of the world.

Finally, the values and attitudes developed by a comprehensive geography scheme of work should be noted. As with many other subjects, geography fosters inter-personal skills. It also helps children to develop the associated values of:

1. Respect for the views of others.
2. Respect for evidence.
3. Empathy for people with other cultures, lifestyles and beliefs.
4. Awareness of bias, prejudice and intolerance.
5. Respect and concern for the Earth.
6. Willingness to become actively involved in caring for the Earth at the local and global scales.

As Wiegand states:

The starting point for the development of positive attitudes to other nationalities is the development of sensitivity and thoughtfulness in the classroom. .... Concepts such as co-operation , conflict, fairness and interdependence need to be built in a classroom context.... (Wiegand, 1993).

Later he claims:

There are at least two inescapable values that teachers must actually teach towards: firstly that the study of people's interrelationship with the environment is necessary and worthwhile; and secondly that experience of environments enriches human existence and therefore we must teach towards an interest in and concern for the quality of environments.

In conclusion, without geography (and its associated humanities subject history), there is no spatial or temporal context in which to study the world and its civilisations. Without these there is no civilisation.

Key Issue 3: Geography and Cross Curricular Themes and Links

One of the reasons for geography's problems associated with topic-focused learning is its traditional role as a 'bridge' subject. Geography has been seen as the link between the sciences and the arts, although Blyth and Krause (1995) see it, somewhat unrealistically, more as the bridge of a ship from where the whole curriculum is navigated (see Figure 1.3). Geography's schizophrenia is the source of its strengths and weaknesses, at all levels. At the research level its interests are served (or ignored?) by a bewildering number of

Research Councils: at the level of government funding it is unclear as to whether geography is a science or art. In some countries (such as the USA) it barely exists as a distinct subject. In the school curriculum its versatility has allowed it to make worthwhile contributions to many topics and to be a vehicle and context for many skills and teaching methods such as observation, recording, measurement, simulation, problem solving, decision making and role plays. In addition, its knowledge base in the arts, social sciences and sciences has meant that its contribution to the whole curriculum is potentially immense, yet unfortunately it is frequently superficial. Finally, its locational emphasis provides all other disciplines with a spatial context for their studies, as Haworth for the Brontë sisters.

Stemming from its role as a bridge subject, geography has much to offer the five cross curricular themes of Economic and Industrial Understanding (National Curriculum Council, 1990b), Health Education (NCC, 1990d), Careers

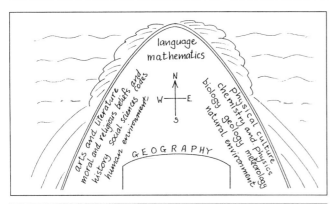

Figure 1.3 Geography as a subject 'bridge'.

Children's visual images of a 'sick world' can stimulate a range of learning activities for everyone.

Education (NCC, 1990a), Environmental Education (NCC, 1990c; Council for Environmental Education, 1994) and Citizenship (NCC, 1991a, Tidy Britain Group, 1993) – see Supplementary Materials 3. The contribution of geography to cross curricular themes has been discussed in detail by Foley and Janikoun (1992) and, despite the Dearing changes, their conclusion that all these themes have a strong relationship with geography remains valid, particularly with regard to environmental education where the role of geography has been strengthened (Chambers, 1995).

It is not the intention here to discuss in detail the links between geography and the other core and foundation subjects. However, a number of general points may be made.

Firstly, there must now be some confusion between the Key Stage 2 teacher who has adopted a child centred view of the curriculum, in which subjects are used to enrich the whole education of the pupils, and the teacher who sees him/herself as a subject specialist who is concerned to teach the subject to children. Official (HMI, DFE, OFSTED, SCAA, NCC) views on this matter change annually; the current one supports the subject-orientated approach.

Secondly, it helps pupils little and teachers even less to become involved in inter-subject claims for curriculum territory. What is required is efficient whole curriculum planning which brings the richness and breadth of a variety of subject approaches and knowledge, without tedious and unnecessary repetition and superficiality.

Thirdly, it is helpful to identify the contribution which geography can make across the curriculum, and this is done in the following sections.

Geography and Science

Geography has long been seen as both a science and an art. Discussion about the science content within the geography National Curriculum has been vigorous, particularly as regards the weather and the hydrological cycle, rocks, weathering, soil, ecology – the study of the inter-relationship between plants and animals and the physical environment. It is also noteworthy that both science and geography involve similar methods of investigation and practical study of phenomena in the field and the laboratory (Trend, 1995). However, a major distinction between science and geography can be recognised in terms of the spatial and human elements in geography which are not central to science.

Practical weather study across the geography/science boundary.

Geography, Information Technology and Design and Technology

Geography is closely related to information technology (IT) and design and technology. Links between geography and IT are discussed in detail in Chapter 3. Design and technology is very much concerned with the application of knowledge and skills to the solution of (technological) problems. This approach to education corresponds very much with the problem solving approaches used by the geographer in geographical enquiry. Equally, geography is related to Nuffield Science for the design and use of appropriate equipment for measuring weather, so much of design and technology is similarly related. There is a 3-way relationship here which can be profitably exploited for children's learning. In addition, the processes and systems used in technology have major application to the design of settlements, the solution of environmental problems and the management of threats to the environment.

Geography and Mathematics

As regards mathematics, the role of geography is to contextualise and make relevant the data collection, recording, presentation, analysis and interpretation of the mathematician. So, the counting and classification of vehicles can have purpose other than the production of histograms and pictograms, and the floating of 'Pooh sticks' beneath bridges can have a purpose other than its enjoyment or its ability to develop children's concepts of time and distance. Mathematics has much to offer children's learning in geography as it refines, for example, fieldwork observations, questionnaire surveys or the analysis of census data.

Children's developing understanding on coordinates and of maps as representations of spatial distribution is best developed by linking mathematics and geography.

Geography and History

Despite the perceived closeness of geography and history, the link in National Curriculum terms is relatively weak, apart from the history study units on (i) local history and (ii) Ancient Greece or past non-European societies. With local history, it is possible to examine the local area from both a historical and geographical perspective using a wide range of interrelated resources, including maps and censuses. With ancient societies, it is possible to study, for example, Greece, Egypt, Mexico or Nigeria from both historical and geographical points of view (Chambers and Donert, 1995), thus saving time and effort whilst avoiding arbitrary academic subdivisions such as time and space distinctions. In addition, the enquiry methods of geography and history share many similarities.

Geography, English, Art and Music

Other arts subjects such as English, art and music can usefully contribute to children's learning in geography through the use of:

1. Speaking and listening.
2. Reading and writing.
3. Mapping.
4. Drawing, painting, printmaking.
5. Collage and sculpture.
6. Textiles.

in order to describe, model and capture the spirit of places and events. Conversely, geography provides contexts in which the art and music of cultures across the world can be studied and appreciated (Chambers and Donert, 1995).

Finally the challenge of outdoor and adventurous physical and problem solving activities in physical education forms an important ingredient in all fieldwork. The need for pupils in geography to understand how people affect the environment (during their recreation) and how and why people seek to manage and sustain their environment can also be associated with outdoor education and fieldwork.

Geography and the European Union

At a time when the links between the United Kingdom and the European Union have been strengthened, many people have been surprised that there is no requirement to include the study of Europe in the Key Stage 2 geography NC. This omission no doubt relates to curriculum overload at Key Stage 2 and to the politically stronger demands of the multicultural and development studies lobbies. At the Dearing reorganisation, room for the European Union was made by re-writing in the expectation that the contexts for the four geographical themes should include the European Union.

Key Issue 4: Special Educational Needs

Geography Needs Special Needs

After over twenty years' teaching one of the present authors has three abiding fieldwork memories:

Abdul (a wheelchair student) driving across a Welsh farm in his adapted car, getting out, and carrying out the fieldwork in his wheel chair ... and Anna (a profoundly deaf student) dedicating and singing *Everything I am* ... to my colleagues and me on the last night of a glaciation field trip in the French Alps ... and Gareth (a very backward, tough and disturbed pupil) from my wife's special needs unit at a Morriston comprehensive school, sitting still for almost an hour in the Gower Peninsula looking at flowers and their different parts.

In its review of inspection findings for 1993/94 OFSTED reported that, with respect to provision for pupils with special educational needs, "most primary schools were meeting statutory requirements for the geography Order" (OFSTED, 1995). At least some of this success must be attributed to the publications of the Geographical Association and the National Association for Remedial Education and leading authors such as Jackie Dilkes (1988) and Judy Sebba (1991;1995).

What are Special Educational Needs?

The Warnock Report (1978) estimated that 20% of pupils would have special educational needs at some time in their school lives and that at any one time the proportion of children with special needs was 16%. Most of these children are accommodated in ordinary schools. Approximately 2% are 'statemented' and provision is made for some of these in special schools where four main groups can be identified:

1. Those with moderate learning difficulties.
2. Those with severe learning difficulties.
3. Those who are emotionally and behaviourally disturbed.
4. Others.

There are two main groups of children with special educational needs (s.e.n.):

1. Those who suffer from physical disabilities such as hearing, vision and mobility.
2. Slow learners.

As Smith (1988) says,

It is difficult to write in general terms about any group of handicapped (sic) children, especially as some handicaps can vary on a daily basis and according to personality, intelligence and home difficulties.....Work must be carefully planned with stages and methods needed to achieve objectives as close to 'normal' as possible. These are not just academic but social, emotional and physical as well. Geography can contribute to all these fields.

Since the 1988 Education Reform Act pupils with special educational needs share a common entitlement to a broad and balanced curriculum with their peers. Special educational needs range from a minority of pupils with profound and multiple disabilities to the majority of pupils with difficulties of a mild, moderate or temporary kind (NCC, 1989). Since this latter group are in the majority it is important to note how ordinary schools are going to ensure that the whole curriculum is accessible to them. NCC (1989) recommends that the school development plan should ensure that:

1. All staff know which pupils have special educational needs.
2. Maximum access and progress for pupils with special educational needs are possible.
3. Adequate resources, support and training are available to staff.
4. A designated member of staff is responsible for coordinating school wide s.e.n. policy.
5. The effects of the National Curriculum on pupils with s.e.n. can be monitored and evaluated.

Geography's Contribution in Special Needs

There is no doubt that geography has much to offer s.e.n.

pupils. Serf (1988) refers to the 'Transportation Theory', where "geography is a great vehicle for the teaching of children with learning problems. Most children find the subject matter intrinsically interesting, and of course, its widespread use of visual aids and fieldwork offers great potential."

Similarly, Judy Sebba (1991) says, when discussing children with learning difficulties, "geography offers tremendous scope through practical activities in and out of the classroom."

Many teachers can give examples of children with little academic success coming alive and gaining self-respect when put into a practical, problem solving or physical environment. The following views of the NCC (1989) with regard to science are equally applicable to fieldwork in geography, especially physical geography:

Science has particular characteristics which mean that pupils with difficulties in other areas of learning can still achieve success. For example
1. *It emphasises firsthand experience – reading and writing difficulties are therefore less inhibiting.*
2. *Knowledge and skills can be acquired in small, manageable steps through practical activity, so helping concentration.*
3. *Scientific investigations can capture the imagination and help to reduce behavioural problems.*

Challenges to Geography in Special Needs Teaching

Not all geography is readily accessible to s.e.n. pupils. It must be recognised that "the areas of the geography curriculum that are hardest to access are generally those which are most difficult to present though active means" (Sebba, 1991).

These include contrasting and distant locality studies and some abstract aspects about the 'sense of place'. In such situations it is necessary for teachers to utilise the full range of techniques described by Sebba as nine principles (see the next section) which include the use of story, drama and simulations and CD-ROM technology. The question of home locality is also difficult because of the widespread practice of transporting s.e.n. pupils considerable distances to their school. As a result, they usually come from a much wider geographical area than is the norm for the class and therefore do not share their experiences of the immediate locality.

General learning difficulties for s.e.n. children are numerous and all will impinge on geographical learning as they do on all other areas of the curriculum. Most serious is language, but others include:

> 1. A lack of experiences either due to overprotection, lack of mobility or lack of visual or hearing skills.
> 2. Poorly developed motor skills.
> 3. Poor social and communication skills.

All handicapped children have a common problem in language development due to their physical experience being limited in some way. Physically handicapped children who have not been able to suck and handle objects, crawl and toddle at normal developmental stages do not have a library of experiences upon which to draw when developing language (Smith, 1988).

The teacher's first priority for pupils who experience language difficulties is to reduce their stress. Frequent informal chats and reinforcement of their listening, talking and comprehension skills in small and structured steps is helpful in achieving this. As with all children, it is important to create favourable conditions for good talking and listening (Mills, 1988). This is achieved through providing:

> 1. Something to talk about.
> 2. Someone to talk to.
> 3. Someone to listen to.
> 4. An atmosphere in which children feel able to talk.

The development of geographical vocabulary can follow, initially focusing on direction and geographical features. Further language skills related to environmental quality and place can be developed by comparing the immediate locality with others using firsthand experience, photographs, videos, posters, artefacts and sound recordings.

A variety of stimulating resources relevant to the current topic, regularly used and frequently changed not only develops the language and communication skills of pupils with special educational needs but also enhances their geographical understanding (Smith and Richardson, 1995).

Similarly, a lack of mobility may have limited children's experiences or vision, as may the possibility of overprotection at home where they may not have had so much outdoor or challenging play as other children. It is essential that the children are challenged as much as is reasonably possible through a range of experiences so as to ensure maximum

stimulation and associated language and conceptual development. Usually this can be achieved easily, since much of the work undertaken with s.e.n. pupils is in groups which are often small enough to allow them to be transported. This enables these children to have experiences beyond the classroom on a regular basis (Blyth and Krause, 1995).

Problems of vision are more fundamental to geography since so much learning is based on firsthand and visual experience. However, careful planning and frequent exposure to stimuli can help, and there are many resources such as Braille writing, compasses, maps, and globes which are designed to be used by tactile means. Audio tapes are other important resources.

Hearing difficulties are less crucial to learning through geography, although deaf pupils may have a limited vocabulary. Difficulty in social intercourse and the lack of hearing may present safety problems in some fieldwork situations.

A lack of development of motor skills and physical coordination are potentially serious handicaps for fieldwork activities. The range of problems is immense but the involvement of severely handicapped children in challenging outdoor education activities, including abseiling, should serve as an inspiration to those wishing to extend geographical fieldwork to all. Where this is not possible a range of group activities should be available so that the physically handicapped child is not singled out. Away from fieldwork, physical handicap need not be such a problem, as it can be for subjects like science, because sensitivity of motor skills is not so crucial for health and safety: map drawing and graphicacy can be replaced with three dimensional modelling. Even with science-based activities, safety need not be an insurmountable barrier. With experience and training, pupils with visual impairment can use much the same equipment that is used by their peers. With practice, electronic equipment, scalpels and glassware can be handled safely. Pupils with a physical disability and those with learning difficulties can be taught to understand safety procedures so they can work safely and with confidence (NCC, 1989).

Increasing Children's Access to Geography

As mentioned above, Sebba (1995) identified nine principles for increasing children's access to geography. Teachers should:

> 1. Seek relevance, for example, through focusing on people or homes. →

2. Develop activities which take account of pupils' interests and experiences.

3. Take every opportunity to use geographical language across the curriculum, for example, at the simplest level, 'up/down', 'in front of', 'near' and 'far'.

4. Look for opportunities to address pupils' individual priorities within geographical activities, for example, communication skills or mobility within fieldwork activities.

5. Use a variety of resources, for example, videos, objects, photographs, maps, other people, buildings and sites.

6. Vary the teaching approaches as much as possible, using drama, information technology, and working individually, in pairs, small groups or whole class.

7. Share the purposes of sessions with pupils.

8. Invite pupils to record information, responses, and reflections, using drawings, photographs, symbols, computers or cassette recorders, as appropriate.

9. Use total communication such as symbols, signing, and Braille to increase pupils' access to activities.

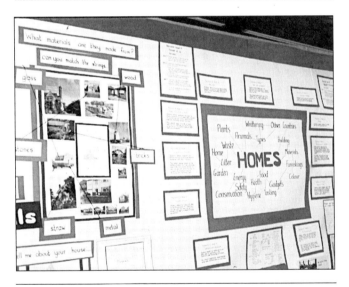

Increasing childrens' access by focusing on direct experiences: 'Homes'.

Most of these principles will benefit all pupils, not just those with identified learning difficulties. 'Ordinary geography' has much to learn from 's.e.n. geography' with the emphasis on the tailoring of work to individual needs (differentiation), the wide range of teaching and learning techniques used (particularly those which are practical and not dependent on the written word), the use of small groups, frequent trips and ensuring small steps in learning.

Key Issue 5: Themes, Places and Localities

Geography Units: Place- or Theme-Based?

As Foley and Janikoun (1992) note, "of all the aspects of National Curriculum geography, it is place that has caused most controversy."

Despite certain reservations, Wendy Morgan (1993; 1995) has no real doubt that place-based geography at Key Stages 1 and 2 is the most appropriate:

A place-based structure is strongly recommended for Key Stages 1 and 2 .... This emphasises the importance of studying real places in geography, while providing a convenient framework in which to plan the coverage of map work, physical, human and environmental geography (Morgan, 1993).

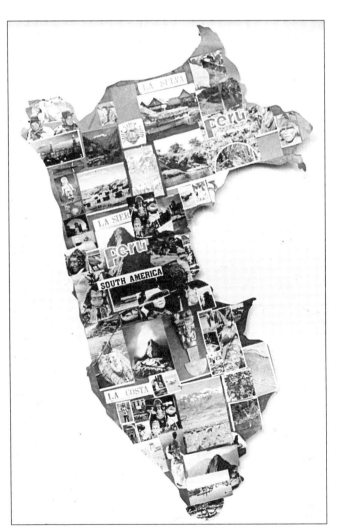

Effective use of collage to show images and the country outline.

Many primary teachers, as already noted, work within topic contexts. Unless specifically trained in geography, many would not make use of Wendy Morgan's locality-based approach. They are often far more comfortable with themes such as *People who help us*, *Transport* or *Volcanoes* than they are with *A Locality in St Lucia*. In the last fifty years or so, academic geographers have abandoned the regional approach in favour of the systematic or thematic approach. Prior to the National Curriculum a primary teacher was far more inclined to study topics such as *Homes* and perhaps use examples from a range of different (stereotyped?) places than focus on homes (and other topics) in one particular locality (see Figure 1.4). Similarly an academic geographer might study the theme of housing on a global scale and look for patterns and generalisations rather than look at a sequence of individual unique case studies which, taken together, reveal patterns.

The 'case for place' or more precisely 'people in places' in geography at Key Stage 2 is that:

1. Places are real, with definable boundaries.
2. Children exist physically and socially in particular places.
3. Children can empathise with children in other places.

The problem with 'place' is that children tend to develop information and understanding of a narrow range of unique places (albeit concentrically nested and carefully chosen by the teacher to reflect specific economic and cultural features), with little appreciation of pattern, generality and frequency of their repetition.

Despite the general preference for place-based units, some teachers prefer the theme-based approach:

Focusing on places is only one way in which the geography curriculum can be organised. Some schools choose to focus on the thematic material and cover the place component by occasional visits to specified localities (Morgan 1993).

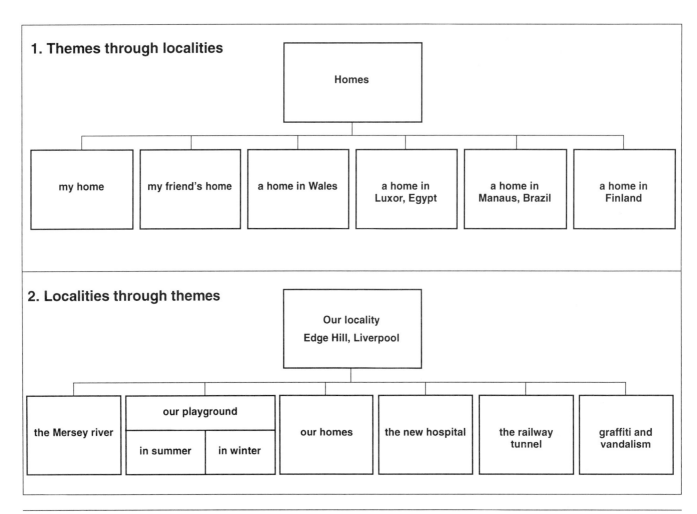

Figure 1.4 Geography units: place- or theme-based?

The themes of rivers, weather, settlement and environmental change can be studied whilst employing a range of contrasting localities to exemplify them. So, for example, it is possible to study a local stream, a contrasting UK river (the Severn, Thames and Trent are named on Map A in the National Curriculum, but others of more local relevance would do), a European Union river (again the Rhine is named on Map B but others such as the Rhone or Danube would suffice), and a river in Africa, Asia, South America or Central America and the Caribbean (the Amazon and Nile are named on Map C). What is important is that the rivers should be set within the context of actual places and people and the learning should be topical. It would be possible, though it is not recommended, to study the whole geography curriculum through rivers!

What is clear, however, is that the geography curriculum should not be taught through skills. Children's manipulative and intellectual skills in geography should be developed within the theme- or locality-based studies. Topics such as mapwork or fieldwork should not normally be seen as free standing but as services to the content-based topics.

A lively display which gives coherence to key geographical features through 'Our Street'.

Your Locality or Mine?

At an early stage in the evolution of the National Curriculum it was appreciated that children at Key Stages 1 and 2 operated within a relatively small geographical space. Their 'personal' geographies were limited to a geographical area in which they and their friends lived, played and went to school. At an equally early stage in the National Curriculum's evolution it was suggested that a small island was an appropriately sized place to study and that, with its clearly defined boundaries, the limits to the locality would be apparent to all. Seen by some as a sop to academic geographers, consideration was given at Key Stage 2 to the concept of a region through the designation of The Home Region. However the emphasis remained on the small scale locality in the study of foreign places.

As Catling (1995) indicates, the Dearing revision defined the locality as an area which is based on and around a rural or urban community. For children in Key Stage 1 this may be the immediate environs of the school. At Key Stage 2 its definition was widened to comprise an area larger than the immediate vicinity of the school, to include the homes of the majority of the pupils. In addition, the broader geographical context of all localities should be referred to, thus allowing the inclusion of broader town, regional or national contexts in all locality studies. In many ways this represents a confirmation of what most good geography teachers had done previously. Since rarely would they consider a locality isolated from its broader geographical context, expressed in terms of the region in which it is located, the surrounding countries and large scale physical features such as oceans and mountain ranges. The narrow, context free view of a locality was, in its own way, a mirror of the abstract and generalised 'typical village in Peru' approach which was so strongly criticised by the original National Curriculum Working Party when it insisted, quite rightly, on the use of real localities, people and families in case studies.

Key Issue 6: Geography Fieldwork; More than Safety and Cash

We start with three quotations from a recent OFSTED document (1995).

Many schools provided a structured programme of local and distant visits, some residential, during which pupils frequently achieved good standards of work.

Personal investigative work through field visits had a positive impact on standards; this work brought about enthusiasm for the subject and motivation to present work well.

More opportunities should be taken for investigative work and fieldwork in the school grounds and locally, as well as further afield.

Of all the skills that a geography-orientated student teacher can take to a job interview, the ability to plan, manage and follow up a field trip in a safe and academically rigorous manner is probably one of the most useful she/he can offer to a school. This is the geographer's equivalent of playing the piano at assembly, running the school pantomime or organising sports day.

Fieldwork probably results in the most exciting and academically memorable events in the lives of many children (Figure 1.5), whether it be undertaken in the school, its grounds, the locality, the town, the region, a contrasting locality or a foreign locality, and whether it be for a few minutes, a day or a week's residential visit. Increasingly, however, fieldwork is coming under pressure because of the dual demands of funding and safety. Local management of schools means that every trip must be fully justified and, preferably, included in a whole school fieldwork plan, since

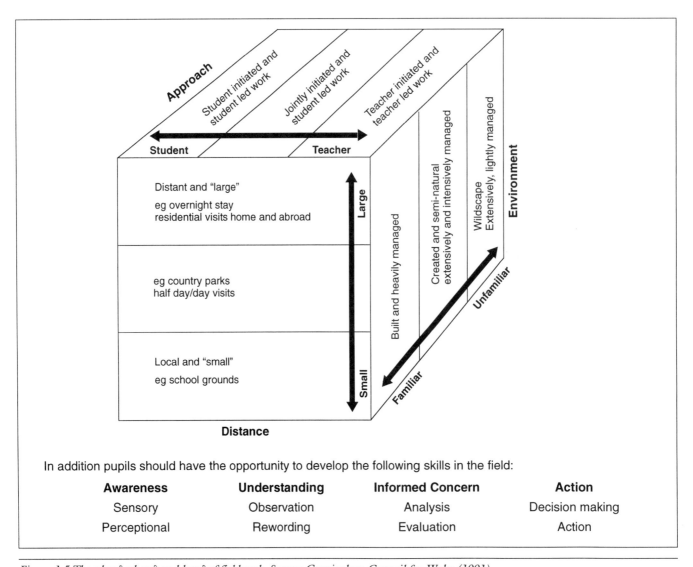

Figure 1.5 The when? where? and how? of fieldwork. Source: Curriculum Council for Wales (1991).

'Look and See' can form part of a much wider range of fieldwork experiences.

Purposes of fieldwork: theirs or the teacher's?

scarce resources are invested in such activities. Similarly, the need for safety, whether it be in the school minibus (with seat belts) or at the field site itself, is paramount. Financial arrangements for field trips constitute another potential minefield. Professional organisations such as the teacher unions offer useful advice on this and other matters, as does a recent publication by Booth et al (1993).

Fieldwork offers the opportunity for interesting and innovative teaching and learning. There is far more to it than the traditional 'Cook's Tour' or 'Look and See' approaches. Enquiry methods and problem solving are centrally important in fieldwork, as is experience in the design and use of equipment. Whether it is labelled science or geography, the design of an investigation, the collection and analysis of data involve important skills and, naturally, take place largely in the field, the 'geographer's laboratory' (See Figure 1.6).

Fieldwork, of course, includes far more than the narrow academic study of a river or a farm. Equally important are the social and physical challenges of fieldwork (Figure 1.7). Despite the increase in out of classroom activities at Key Stage 1, geography fieldwork represents, for many Key Stage 2 pupils, the first time that they have worked outside the classroom. In particular, with day trips and residential experiences, it is often the first time they have had the opportunity to interact intensively with their peers at a social level for an extended period of time. This means that fieldwork provides social as well as academic management challenges for the teacher, in addition to the financial and safety issues.

Fieldwork remains one of the most challenging and rewarding of activities for teachers and pupils alike and is, furthermore, a formal requirement of the National Curriculum.

Fieldwork 'Look and See': Teacher dominates pupils' learning.

Teacher:	Pupils:	Environment:

Knows & shows	look
	listen
	draw
	observe
	photograph
	walk
	tour
	trail
	collect
	record
	
	might
	meet the
	  Mayor
	  planner
	  landlord
	  shopkeeper
		old & new
		continuity & change
		function
		land use
		features
		similarity & difference

Fieldwork 'Enquiry': Pupils in control of their learning.

Teacher asks:	Pupils focus on:	Environment:
What do you think? How could you? How would you solve? What would it be like?	enquiry questions hypotheses problems issues role play empathy	the new zebra crossing litter problem disabled access

Figure 1.6 Fieldwork 'Look and See' and 'Enquiry'.

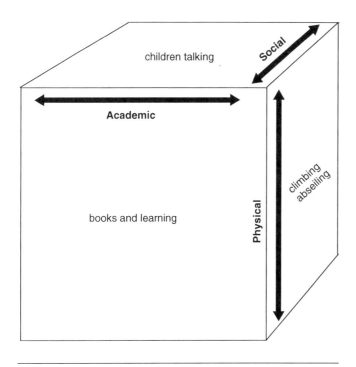

children talking

Social

Academic

climbing
abseiling

Physical

books and learning

Figure 1.7 The benefits of fieldwork.

Key Issue 7: Using Other Adults

The use of parents and other adults in schools and classrooms has progressed a long way since the days when they were seen either as a threat to the class teacher or as a way of raising money for the school fund. Many parents are now school governors and, in some situations, are part of a partnership (eg Liverpool City Council's Parent School Partnership Scheme) in which their skills, experiences and interests in their children can be harnessed for the mutual benefit of the school, the teachers, the pupils and the parents. Adults may become involved with children's learning both within the school and during fieldwork sessions.

Adults as Facilitators and Enhancers

Adults can both facilitate and enhance the learning experiences of children in school and in the field. Whilst some of these processes relate to the whole school curriculum, several are specific to geography.

'Facilitating' adults are those who may be used to make up the staff:pupil ratio or who may use their contacts to allow

a field visit to take place. 'Enhancing' adults are those who may improve the quality of the visit, through the provision of information, expertise or resources.

The visit to school of 'people who help us' has long been a feature of the infant (KS1) curriculum whilst the junior (KS2) curriculum often includes visits from 'experts'. These experts include people such as:

1. The local jeweller to talk about gems in geology.
2. Someone from an organisation which works in the environment, such as *The Tidy Britain Group*.
3. Someone from a distant locality.
4. Travellers to talk about their experiences overseas.

Sometimes visitors from a site or field centre to be visited later in the term come to the school in order to introduce the visit or topic.

The majority of enhancing adults meet the children out of the classroom and school. Many of these are found at the site to be visited where they may be employed or they give their time freely. At its simplest, the enhancing adult is the parent or friend of the school with an interest or specialism which can enhance learning. The builder, the park keeper, the farmer, the publican and the road sweeper are all used. Alternatively, the parent or friend with the knowledge and enthusiasm to lead a locality study field trip may be used. The local authority or private enterprise employee such as the planner or shop manager may often be able to provide resources, insights and unusual perspectives. A local environmental organisation may be able to provide a different perspective on a local issue, or equipment, ideas and access to external environmental projects (with or without funding and publicity). At a more formal level, many organisations provide support of a commercial or public relations nature from professionals or paid employees so that the visit to the power station, country park or urban farm becomes mutually beneficial. Local politicians are also useful in giving a sense of reality to any local project in a way that many teachers may be unable to do.

'Problem' Adults

Whilst 'adults other than teachers' may bring new and real skills and insights, the majority lack teaching expertise. They tend to be either (i) enthusiastic or bored amateurs or (ii) professionals. Either group may suffer from similar problems, such as the following:

1. They are inaudible or they speak too quickly.
2. They are incomprehensible because they assume prior knowledge or use complex language.
3. They talk for too long.
4. They see their role as the transmission of knowledge and facts.
5. They tell children things, rather than encourage them to think.
6. Their resources are inappropriate in that they are too small or too complicated.
7. They are boring because they are poor communi‐cators or because they are bored by repeating the same performance several times per day.

In such a situation it is essential for the teacher to manage the experience, even if it involves a difficult or sensitive approach to the adult concerned. Of fundamental importance is the need for preparation prior to the visit. Children should:

1. Be clear as to where they are going.
2. Know what the relevance of the visit is to them.
3. Be encouraged to prepare questions.
4. Be trained to listen to answers given by the adult.

The enhancing adults should be very clear as to how their contribution fits into the school curriculum or scheme of work. Wherever possible the content of their presentation and the methods to be used should be agreed with the teacher beforehand, so that the method is not simply the talk or the unimaginative crocodile trail around the locality. However, it should be recognised that many organisations have standard inputs which are fixed and non-negotiable.

Employees of such organisations may be either unable or unwilling to customise their input, however unsatisfactory this may be from a school's perspective. Similarly such people may have done the presentation so often that it becomes a sterile and boring experience for provider and pupil.

Managing Experts

Two basic management approaches are useful with the experts, the 'village idiot' and the 'agent provocateur' (Figure 1.8). In 'village idiot' mode the teacher identifies all the omissions, assumptions, irrelevancies and complexities of the adult's presentation and seeks to clarify them by asking basic and simple questions in a structured and ordered sequence. Spellings may be asked for, summaries requested or given, and areas of confusion clarified. The teacher not only provides the structure for the adult but also asks the questions that the children may be reticent to ask.

With the 'agent provocateur' role the teacher acts in a more confrontational manner. This is particularly the case when the visit is contentious or involves a local controversial issue. Here the teacher disagrees with the speaker or puts alternative points of view. Whilst ostensibly challenging the speaker it is also attempting to stimulate the pupils into a questioning and sceptical mode of thought.

Obviously, for both these approaches it is important to inform the adult beforehand and to seek their agreement!

The 'Village Idiot'	The 'Agent Provocateur'
'I don't understand'	'I've never heard that before.'
'Can you say that again slowly please?'	'Most of my friends would not agree with you.'
'Did you say that ...?'	'If I said I disagreed, what would you say?'
'When I was at school ...?'	'Last time we came here somebody said completely the opposite to what you are telling us.'
'Am I right in thinking that ...?'	
'This might seem obvious to you but ...'	'Would you say that if you weren't employed here?'
'I know I'm the only one who doesn't understand but ...'	'On the news the other day it was reported that your factory was ...'
'Could you spell that for me please?'	'If you weren't a planner what would you say?'
	'Councillors always say that, but you don't really listen.'

Figure 1.8 Two approaches to dealing with experts.

Controversial issues: a child's picture to show the impact of environmental pollution.

Key Issue 8: Teaching Controversial Environmental Issues

A common and popular approach to the teaching of geography and environmental education is through real issues. By definition, 'issues' are real, important and immediate. This makes them exciting and motivating themes for study. They exist at all scales from the global to the local: from global warming, the ozone hole and the loss of animal species and habitats to the new bypass, the new supermarket and the cutting down of a local tree. In many ways the mundane local issue offers an opportunity for a full study involving the use of a range of resources, from old maps, newspaper articles, the planning notification to councillors, and a range of people such as environmentalists, developers, planners, tree surgeons, parents and pupils. This allows the development of skills and attitudes which may run in sequence as follows:

1. Awareness of the issue.
2. Identifying the key interest groups.
3. Understanding the different points of view.
4. Identifying their value positions.
5. Proposing various solutions.
6. Evaluation of the proposals.
7. The personal involvement and actions of the pupils.

An issues-based curriculum encourages the development of the full range of English skills from speaking and listening through to reading and writing in a meaningful context.

Involvement in issues inevitably leads to the need for the clarification and application of values and attitudes. A potential problem is the risk of involvement in real controversy, conflict, militancy and indoctrination. Whilst such controversy is usually a mirror of the real world for which children are being prepared, this degree of controversy is not generally acceptable to parents and governors. There are a number of approaches to such problems described in the next 3 paragraphs.

The first must be to gain acceptance for the inclusion of such controversial issues in the school geography curriculum. If support is needed it is necessary to look no further than the National Curriculum Settlement theme (9c) where we are required to ensure that our pupils are taught about a particular issue arising from the way in which land is used, or the Environmental Change theme (10b) where children are to be taught how and why people seek to manage and sustain their environment. Another alternative is the Places section (5d) where we are expected to teach pupils about recent or proposed changes in the localities.

A second approach is to ensure that a balanced view of the issue is presented to the children. This does not necessarily mean that the teacher should remain neutral but rather that opportunities are offered to people from all points of view to put their case.

A third approach is to use the opportunity to identify and draw out the values implicit in each person's attitude and point of view. In this way a logical and rational discussion can be stimulated in which different points of view may be justified (Council for Environmental Education, 1994).

Key Issue 9: Real Resources, or Death by a Thousand Worksheets?

The resourcing of geography was of variable quality, and ranged from very good to poor. Some schools had made considerable investment in atlases, maps, photographs and reference books and used them well. In others, resources were inappropriate or non-existent, and at times the poor storage of resources restricted their use ... a number of schools utilised their own classrooms, buildings, grounds and the local area to good effect, and some had well established visits further afield, including residential courses at Key Stage 2 (OFSTED, 1995).

Good quality work was often associated with the use of 'real' resources such as photographs, maps and experiences of places through films and reference books (OFSTED, 1995).

Real Resources

Without resources a teacher has nothing but wits and voice. Whilst these, plus the associated chalk and talk, may have been perfectly adequate for Miss Jean Brodie and *la crème de la crème* (although we doubt it!), they offer few opportunities for exciting and realistic learning in geography in the 1990s. In many ways "resources maketh the teacher". It is the resources which take children beyond the knowledge and experience of the teacher to the whole world. It is resources which allow a wide range of teaching and learning opportunities. In the absence of first hand experience it is resources which bring geography to life. Good resources encourage interest and increase motivation and allow the development of a wide range of geographical and other skills.

Geography is a highly visual subject and involves children in the study of places, issues and themes which should be "topical" (DFE, 1995) and up to date. Children's expectations of high quality visual presentation of materials plus the need for up to date items means that resources are expensive for publishers to produce and they need frequent revision.

Experimentation and exploration with physical resources fosters sound learning and understanding for most children.

If the Key Stage 2 geography Order is interpreted minimalistically, thematic studies such as rivers and weather are unlikely to change from year to year. However, the same cannot be said about Environmental Change (where nothing dates like yesterday's issues) and Settlements and Places (where land use, population and issues change continuously). Sebba (1995) warns that materials tied specifically to the current requirements may be unlikely to stand the test of time, given the regular revisions which are anticipated.

The authors of two recent guides for teaching primary geography are agreed on the need for resourcing: "The adequate resourcing of the primary curriculum is of fundamental concern to all teachers" (Blyth and Krause, 1995). "To teach primary geography well a wide range of resources is necessary" (Foley and Janikoun, 1992).

The uniqueness of the home locality of each school, the need to use real places and real people, plus the relative freedom of choice in the rest of the geography curriculum, especially the contrasting localities (cf. the tightly designated history study units), has put extra pressure on the choice and consultative powers of the geography curriculum coordinator. As with all resource acquisition, the opinions and expertise of the whole school staff should be used, but the knowledge and opinion of the geography coordinator will remain vitally important.

Worksheets

There was some over-use of worksheets, which were not geared to individual needs and which frequently limited opportunities for extended writing ... There was too much inappropriate use of worksheets, and too much time was spent copying text and diagrams from books (OFSTED, 1995).

Clearly death by a thousand worksheets has reached the primary classroom after years in the secondary school, probably for the same reasons:

1. The teaching of geography by people not trained in the subject and therefore lacking confidence who are happy to take refuge in other people's worksheets.
2. The availability of excellent quality commercial photocopiable master sheets to supplement virtually every primary book series and primary education magazines at present being marketed.   →

3. The accessibility of high quality desk top publishing and laser (and colour) printing facilities and expertise in many schools.
4. The increased acceptance of the use of the photo-copier to replace the banda machine.

Whilst using worksheets is a convenient and seductive method of teaching, occupying and extending children, as with all resources they need to be managed carefully and used by professionals in the appropriate context, not as a time or space filler.

Conclusions

The state of Key Stage 2 geography is not good. The status of Key Stage 2 geography is not good. Problems exist in its relations with the whole curriculum and within geography itself, but the fact remains that no other subject looks at the World as a whole, none other is concerned with the spatial organisation of the human and physical environment and none other encompasses both science- and arts-based approaches. Places are different and people are interesting. Geography retains its attractions for children and for many teachers. Geography offers the world so much, but can we help it to live up to its promise? It is up to us, as teachers with a special interest in geography, to maintain and develop this interest using its wide and interesting content and the variety of appropriate teaching methods.

Chapter 2: Interpreting and Implementing the National Curriculum

Section 1: Curriculum Planning

Teachers are rarely helped in their planning of the geography curriculum by the constantly changing advice offered in various quarters. As recently as 1991, multi subject integrated topic work was advocated by the Curriculum Council for Wales (1991): "Geography may be taught within broad topics covering most areas of the curriculum".

By 1995 OFSTED reported that the geographical focus of topic work was often weak because it had been subsumed within broad topics and SCAA was advocating linking work from only a limited range of subjects (SCAA, 1995).

What's Our Curriculum?

It is important to recognise that there is no single geography curriculum. Unlike history, with its carefully specified study units, a considerable degree of freedom has been given to individual teachers to design their own unique geography curriculum. Although some content is specified, the geography curriculum was designed to give schools flexibility when planning the curriculum. Consequently, as Foley and Janikoun (1992) note, a school should be able to tailor a curriculum to fit current practices and build on its strengths. SCAA (1995) suggest that the following "informed and objective" considerations should influence curriculum design for any subject:

1. The school's aims, objectives and policies.
2. A realistic assessment of the time available for teaching.
3. Staff expertise, subject knowledge and familiarity with the subject.
4. The needs, abilities, interests and achievements of the children.
5. The school's resources and accommodation.
6. The teaching opportunities provided by the locality.

There are, of course, many other influences on the geography curriculum, especially the needs, interests and expectations of the pupils and the community in which the school is located. This may be particularly apparent when choosing a distant locality. St. Lucia might be preferred to Chembakolli for a school with a large West Indian community whilst the converse would be true for a school with a local Indian community.

In Liverpool the LEA has invested heavily in the Colomendy Outdoor Education Centre in Wales. Many schools use this as their contrasting UK locality in Year 6 and accordingly build it into their curriculum. Other Liverpool schools choose nearby Southport or Formby as their contrasting locality.

This flexibility provides teachers with considerable freedom and professional choice, but it has brought problems for some. With history, abundant, carefully focused resources have been commercially produced and schools have been accumulating them. By contrast, geography resources have been more widely spread and the freedom of choice has caused difficulties for some teachers.

It is because of the unique situation of each school that many teachers resist the adoption of formula curricula such as those advocated by some local education authorities or by Wendy Morgan in her *Geography in a Nutshell* (1993) and her recent publication *Plans for Primary Geography* (1995).

Levels of Planning

Needless to say, curriculum planning is carried out in different ways by individuals and groups of teachers at different times, stages and levels of detail. Rawling (1992) identifies five planning levels:

1. School.
2. Key stage.
3. Year group.
4. Scheme of work.
5. Lesson.

The Curriculum Council for Wales (1991) also identifies a five level planning hierarchy (see Figure 2.1):

1. Whole school curriculum plan.
2. Geography curriculum plan.
3. Scheme of work for key stages.
4. Scheme of work for units.
5. Lesson plans.

More recently, SCAA (1995) simplifies this to three broad levels of planning:

Long-term planning, which is concerned with producing a broad curriculum framework for each year of Key Stage 2. It reflects the school's curricular aims and policies and the whole staff and governors are involved at different stages of the process.

Medium-term planning, which deals with the details of the programme of work to be taught to each year group and identifies opportunities for assessment and reporting. It involves year group or key stage teachers, often supported by the geography coordinator.

Short-term planning, which is usually carried out individually by class teachers and is used to focus day to day teaching, assessment and reporting.

Units of Work

The Key Stage 2 geography curriculum can be made up of a number of units of work or topics. These may be of variable length but most school topics last for a maximum of half a term. Foley and Janikoun (1992) favour a mixture of unit lengths ranging between two and twelve weeks depending on the scope and nature of the topic. For example, *Transport in Pampagrande* would occupy much less time than would an in depth enquiry into the village of Pampagrande. Such irregularity in length makes whole school planning a complex and fundamental process.

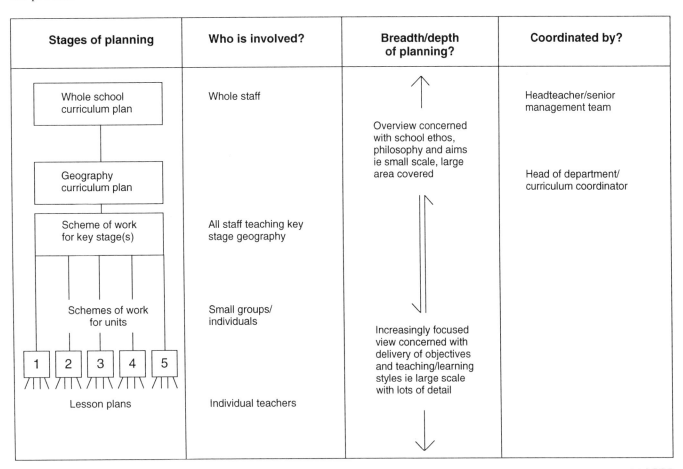

Stages of planning	Who is involved?	Breadth/depth of planning?	Coordinated by?
Whole school curriculum plan	Whole staff	Overview concerned with school ethos, philosophy and aims ie small scale, large area covered	Headteacher/senior management team
Geography curriculum plan			Head of department/ curriculum coordinator
Scheme of work for key stage(s)	All staff teaching key stage geography		
Schemes of work for units	Small groups/ individuals	Increasingly focused view concerned with delivery of objectives and teaching/learning styles ie large scale with lots of detail	
1 2 3 4 5			
Lesson plans	Individual teachers		

Figure 2.1 Planning schemes of work: a planning hierarchy. Source: Curriculum Council for Wales (1991).

Blyth and Krause (1995) favour an arrangement involving a minimum of one substantial geography-based topic each year plus a clearly recognisable geographical component in other topics in each year. They also favour place-based rather than theme-based topics. They identify:

1. Year 3: Nearby places.
2. Year 4: Distant places.
3. Year 5: Distant places (a European place set in France or the Netherlands).
4. Year 6: Our place.

Writing before the Dearing review, Wendy Morgan (1993) advocated seven half-term geography study units, all locality based. In a more recent post Dearing publication (1995) she proposes twelve units each of 15 hours duration:

1. School locality: four units.
2. UK localities: two (one by twinning, the other by residential fieldwork).
3. Overseas locality: visited twice (or two localities).
4. Themes: four units (rivers, weather, settlements and environmental change).

The places and themes are revisited in Years 5 and 6 to ensure progression.

The Northampton Inspection and Advisory Service has developed a thematic approach using six units; three in each of Years 3/4 and 5/6:

1. Places where we live.
2. Services we need.
3. Places where we work.
4. Resources we use.
5. Landscapes where we live.
6. Land we use.

Another important decision which teachers need to make is whether to use a lesson a week throughout the year for geography or to consolidate it into one half-term block. In the experience of the writers the first approach is to be preferred because it ensures a continuous exposure to geography throughout the key stage rather than in intermittent blocks. However Foley and Janikoun (1992) claim that "variety in the duration and depth of units of work and the integration of geography with different subjects at different times should lead to a broad, balanced primary curriculum".

Categories of Unit

There are three main categories of geography work units, *continuing, blocked* and *linked* (SCAA, 1995).

Continuing work comprises that which is largely drawn from geography and which:

1. Requires regular and frequent teaching and assessment to be planned across a year or key stage to ensure progression.
2. Contains a progressive sequence of learning activities.
3. Requires time for the systematic and gradual acquisition, practice and consolidation of skills, knowledge and understanding.
4. Can be developed and/or revisited in other subjects.

Examples of this include map work, although it is not advisable to teach this divorced from a meaningful context. Another example is locational knowledge, where assessment activities relating to the names and locations of places and features can be utilised whenever there is an opportunity. Weather recording is another activity that can be extended throughout the year as a continuing unit so that all children can be given the opportunity to participate. Seasonal differences can be observed, recorded, discussed, explained and so forth.

Blocked work arises from curriculum content which is drawn from geography and which can be taught as a unit within a specified time, not exceeding a term. It focuses on a distinct and cohesive body of knowledge, understanding and skills. It may be taught alone or it may have the potential for linking with units of work in other curriculum areas. Good examples of this include the study of settlements, rivers or weather conditions in other parts of the world.

Linked units involve children's learning in a number of different subjects. There are three good reasons for linking subjects in this way. Firstly, they contain common or complementary areas of knowledge, understanding and skills. This could include the water cycle or environmental change in geography and science; or the school locality or (Ancient) Greece or Egypt as contrasting localities in geography and history.

Secondly, the skills acquired in one subject or aspect of the curriculum can be applied or consolidated in the context of another. For example, work on coordinates in mathematics can be applied to work in geography on grid references. Historical sources such as census data, artefacts and old pictures can enrich and provide a basis for school locality studies. The skills of IT can be used in the collection, analysis and communication of data for a geographical enquiry into traffic counts and building surveys.

Thirdly, work on one subject may provide a stimulus for work in another. For example, writing a poem as a result of studying the natural landscape of the school locality, or making a collage map of a contrasting locality.

The development of linked units is potentially dangerous since it could easily degenerate into the topic webs of the 1980s, constructed through brainstorming and producing impressive lateral thinking but little coherence and focus. SCAA suggest that the design of these units should follow the establishment of a manageable framework of continuing and blocked units. Practising teachers would no doubt add the need for familiarity with single subject approaches before looking for linked units.

Whatever the form of the units, links between individual geography units and between geography units and other parts of the curriculum should be exploited. For example, it may be possible to link units so that each year can have a unifying theme. Looking for similarities and differences between the school locality and a contrasting UK locality can form a unifying strand between thematic topics on weather, rivers, settlements and environmental issues. Alternatively units can be sequenced to draw on knowledge and understanding acquired in previous units. For example, a unit on weather which involves the measurement of rainfall and temperature can be a useful introduction to understanding the weather of a hot, dry distant locality which follows the weather unit. Finally, the timing of topics across the curriculum should take into account complementary knowledge and skills, so you must at an early stage decide whether first to teach coordinates as part of mathematics or geography.

Section 2: Enquiry

The Enquiry Approach

The enquiry method gives a focus to children's learning (see Figure 2.2). A focus means that the pupils are less likely to resort to verbose descriptive accounts of topics and more likely to produce perceptive, focused and analytical studies with a purpose.

Geography

Enquiry is the process of finding out answers to questions. At its simplest, it involves encouraging children to ask questions and search for answers, based on what they might already know and from data sources. As their skills develop, children can move to a more rigorous form of enquiry involving the development and testing of hypotheses. (NCC, 1993)

History: historical enquiry

a. Find out about aspects of the periods studied, from a range of sources of information, including documents and printed sources, artefacts, pictures and photographs, music, buildings and sites;

b. To ask and answer relevant questions, and to select and record information relevant to a topic. (DFE, 1995)

Science: systematic enquiry

a. Ask questions related to their work in science;

b. Use focused exploration and investigation to acquire scientific knowledge, understanding and skills;

c. Use both firsthand and secondary sources to obtain information. (DFE, 1995)

Figure 2.2 Enquiry across the curriculum.

The enquiry approach is process- rather than product-orientated and, although enhanced knowledge and understanding is a normal outcome, a key benefit is that children develop their learning skills: they learn how to learn.

In early versions of the geography National Curriculum, the enquiry approach was important but references were *en passant*. In the Dearing edition the approach is included within geographical skills whereby pupils should be given opportunities to:

1. Observe and ask questions about geographical features and issues.
2. Collect and record evidence to answer the questions.
3. Analyse the evidence, draw conclusions and communicate findings.

The enquiry approach takes children through a sequence of stages:

> 1. Recognising an issue or focus for enquiry.
> 2. Asking a question or series of questions.
> 3. Collecting relevant data from primary and/or secondary sources.
> 4. Analysing and interpreting data.
> 5. Presenting the findings.
> 6. Drawing conclusions.
> 7. Evaluating the enquiry.
> (NCC, 1991)

This is not a rigid sequence.

Enquiries can be of different lengths. A set of questions asked about a photograph could comprise an enquiry taking 15 to 20 minutes, or the enquiry could be the basis of several weeks' work. The enquiry approach could also underpin a scheme of work for the whole key stage (CCW, 1991).

Sometimes only a few stages or questions may be used, such as in short enquiries, as noted by Foley and Janikoun (1992): "the age and experience of the children; the experience of the teacher in using the enquiry process and the time available can be the only guidance for the teacher's professional judgement".

However Morgan (1993) recommends that the full systematic enquiry should take place at least once in each key stage.

Enquiry Questions

Fundamental to a good enquiry is a stimulating topic and a clearly focused and challenging series of questions. Generally it is preferable if the enquiry emerges at least from 'guided discovery' rather than being imposed by the teacher. If the teacher is using an issues-based approach to some aspects of the geography curriculum it is surprising how frequently interesting and relevant issues arise in the local area which then lead to fascinating enquiries (see Figure 2.3). As with much worthwhile work, ownership of the enquiry adds significantly to the quality of interest and work produced by the pupils. Related to ownership of the enquiry is the degree of pupil autonomy in the planning and execution of the process. The NCC Geography INSET Resources (1993) include a grid which plots the Year of the child against the enquiry activity being carried out (see Figure 2.4). For example, the teacher is expected to be responsible for all the activities except collecting, processing and presenting

Exciting issues in boring Woolton Road
Where should the zebra crossing be placed? Do we need a zebra crossing?
Should we allow a new takeaway restaurant instead of the hardware store?
Should Redrow be allowed to cut down eight one hundred year old trees for a new housing estate?
How can we stop our grass verge being eroded by pedestrians?
Should MANWEB be allowed to enlarge the electricity substation?
Should the college be allowed to build a new astroturf pitch behind the houses?

Figure 2.3.

Year	1	2	3	4	5	6
Activity						
Framing questions	T	?	?	?	?	T/C
Planning the investigation	T	T	T	?	?	T/C
Collecting data	C	C	C	C	C	C
Processing data	C/T	?	?	?	?	C
Presenting evidence	C/T	?	?	?	?	?
Drawing conclusions	T	?	?	?	?	?
Evaluating the findings	T	?	?	?	?	T/C

T = teacher responsible   C = child responsible

Figure 2.4 Encouraging children's responsibility in enquiry-based learning. Source: NCC (1993).

data in Year 1. By Year 6 the responsibilities are either shared or rest with the children.

Much discussion in geography has focused on the nature of geographical questions. Since Michael Storm (1989) posed his original 5 questions for the geography of place, many modifications and additions have been made (Catling, 1995; Morgan, 1995; Lewis and Watts, 1995; Foley and Janikoun, 1992; Rawling, 1992), but few share his clarity and brevity:

> 1. What is this place like?
> 2. Why is it like it is?
> 3. How is it connected to other places?
> 4. How is it changing and why?
> 5. What does it feel like to be there?

Morgan (1993) added her own list of questions for themes and processes on which the following is based:

> 1. What is happening?
> 2. Where is it happening?
> 3. What caused it to happen?
> 4. What is the result of the event?
> 5. What will happen in the future?
> 6. What do people think about it?

The study of geography involves the study of issues which have political, social, economic, aesthetic and environmental dimensions. Despite changing attitudes of successive Secretaries of State to an issues-based curriculum (Rawling, 1991), there is no doubt that it offers stimulating contexts for geographical enquiry. For such enquiries the following questions form a useful framework:

1. What is the issue?
2. What are its geographical aspects?
3. Where is the issue taking place?
4. What is the place like?
5. What are the background factors to the issue?
6. What groups and individuals are involved?
7. What views do they hold?
8. What attitudes and values underlie these views?
9. What alternative solutions are there?
10. What are their advantages and disadvantages?
11. What are your feelings about the issue?
12. How will a decision be made?
13. Who will make it?
(CCW, 1991)

Making the Enquiry Stimulating

What is important about enquiries and enquiry questions is that they should interest and stimulate children into learning. Many of the examples published in recent texts equate primary school enquiries with rather simplistic descriptive data collection in response to non stimulating questions. Rawling (1992) identifies this problem when she encourages us to "ensure that geographical work does not just describe and categorise things as they are", and to help children to explore the more challenging questions such as "how they got like that, how they are changing, what impacts and consequences will occur for people, place and environment, what might things be like in the future, and what do I think about it and why?"

Lewis and Watts (1995) are similarly concerned that we should "lead on to questions which are cognitively more demanding and require the child to explain and predict", so they present key questions together with the language skills being developed by each question (see Figure 2.5).

SCAA are also concerned that there should be progression in enquiry skills and in their unpublished briefing notes circulated at INSET sessions during 1995 they drew attention to such progression:

Questions	Skills
What is this?	Naming/identifying
Where is it?	Locating
What is it like?	Describing/comparing
How did it come to be like this?	Explaining
What physical and/or human processes caused it to be like this?	
How might things change?	Predicting/hypothesising
What do I think and feel about this?	Evaluating/caring

Figure 2.5 Key questions and skills.

1. Level 1: responding to questions.
2. Level 2: asking and responding to questions.
3. Level 4: drawing on knowledge and understanding to suggest suitable geographical questions for study.
4. Level 6: drawing on knowledge and understanding to identify relevant geographical questions and suggest appropriate sequences of investigation, ... presenting conclusions which are consistent with the evidence.

Section 3: Progression

Progression is the careful and deliberate sequencing of learning so that children can build their current learning on previous experience and also prepare for future learning. The SCAA Geography Advisory Group (established to review the National Curriculum during 1994) commented that there was "no clear view of progression" and identified the key question as "how should progression be defined?" (Ranger, 1995). "The National Curriculum is intended to support continuity and progression in pupil's learning, through the framework provided by programmes of study and the attainment targets" (Bennetts, 1995).

Level descriptions are summative statements which describe the characteristics of children's achievement at the end of each key stage. The descriptions have been written to represent progression through ten levels.

Progression is important because:

1. It helps avoid unnecessary duplication of work.
2. It helps teachers to maximise the value of teaching by posing such questions as "What existing children's knowledge/experiences/skills does this session make use of?" or "How does this session prepare children for new aspects of learning?"
3. It provides a mechanism for increasing the cognitive abilities of children by providing new and more demanding goals.

(NCC, 1993)

Forms of Progression

Children's progression in knowledge, skills and understanding can be fostered in many different ways. *The INSET Geography Resources* (NCC, 1993) draw heavily on *Geography from 5 to 16* (DES, 1986) and identify eight forms:

1. The level of difficulty of practical and intellectual tasks, eg from using letter/number coordinates to four figure grid references.
2. The breadth of study, eg from studying certain aspects of a local stream to making an analysis of a river network.
3. The depth of study, eg from the local shop and a survey of its produce to an explanation of its source of produce, its customers and sales.
4. The complexity of phenomena studied and tasks set, eg from a short, straightforward journey to school to the study of route networks and transport systems.
5. The range of scales studied, eg from a school locality to its wider geographical context such as the region.
6. The understanding of generalised and abstract matters as opposed to the concrete and specific, eg from rainfall in the school grounds to rainfall patterns in different parts of the world.
7. The awareness of social, political and environmental issues, eg from personal preferences in the locality to conflicting well argued cases for action in the local environment.
8. The range, accuracy and complexity of vocabulary used, eg from 'a valley' to a 'steep-sided v-shaped valley with a narrow flood plain'.

The revised NC Geography document provides five main areas which require careful attention with regard to progression:

1. Pupils' ability to show their knowledge, understanding and skills at a widening range of scales and in contrasting contexts, eg in more distant and less familiar social, economic, climatic and cultural localities.
2. Pupils' ability to draw on a widening range of geographical skills, and use them with increasing selectivity, accuracy and independence eg both enquiry and map work are recurrent skills (see Figure 2.6).
3. A growing understanding of the similarities and differences between places.
4. A growing understanding of human and physical processes in geography and the effects of their interactions.
5. A growing understanding about the ways in which the environmental issues arise and are tackled, eg progression can be identified in the extent to which pupils can give reasons for their preferences, can appreciate the views of others, and have developed some understanding of how peoples' likes and dislikes, beliefs and wants can influence their actions.

(SCAA, 1995)

Level 1	Respond to questions using provided resources and their own observations.
Level 2	Ask and respond to questions using provided resources and their own observations.
Level 3	Use skills and sources of evidence to respond to a range of geographical questions.
Level 4	Suggest suitable geographical questions drawing on their knowledge and understanding.
Level 5	Identify relevant geographical questions drawing on their knowledge and understanding, select and use appropriate skills and evidence to carry out investigation.
Level 6	Identify relevant questions and suggest appropriate sequences of investigation. Select and make effective use of a wide range of skills and evidence to carry out investigation.

Figure 2.6 Progression in questioning in geography

Progression in Fieldwork

Progression in cognitive abilities can be fostered through the judicious use of fieldwork. The Curriculum Council for Wales (1991) identifies the following key areas for progression within fieldwork:

1. Increasing precision and detail in data recording.
2. Increasing sophistication in the analysis and interpretation of the data.
3. Increasing spatial scale and movement from the familiar to the unfamiliar.
4. Increasing complexity of ideas developed and understanding achieved.

4. Geographical ideas and concepts.
5. Issues and problems under investigation.

These areas show more sophisticated methods of data collection; greater precision in recording and presenting data; more independence in the interpretation and analysis of data and more autonomy over the structure and methodology of the fieldwork enquiry as examples of progression.

The Fieldwork Cube (see Figure 1.5, page 14) shows the interrelationships between (i) duration of fieldwork (10 minutes to 1 week), (ii) distance travelled (school grounds to overseas) and (iii) degree of pupil autonomy (teacher initiated and led to student initiated and led).

As an example of the potential for progression within a simple fieldwork activity they describe an enquiry into the best physical site for a tent. Progression is shown in Figure 2.7.

Bland et al (1996) discuss progression in fieldwork and identify five key areas where it can be observed:

Progression in Mapwork

1. Skills and techniques.
2. The difficulty of task and level of supervision.
3. Places and themes.   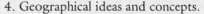

Of all the facets of geography that can illustrate progression, map work is the most straightforward. Whether it is the increase in complexity from four points of the compass to eight, or alphanumeric to numeric grid referencing, children's progression in learning can be clearly demonstrated.

Enquiry into the best physical site for a tent:

Sites:

From ... choice between two sites ... to ... choice between five sites

From ... teacher designates sites ... to ... pupils choose sites to investigate

From ... sites very obviously different (flat/steep slope) ... to ... sites subtly different (flat/gentle slope/medium slope/steep slope)

Observation:

From ... verbal description using small number of contrasted terms (hard/soft) ... to ... large number of differentiated terms (very hard/hard/medium/soft/very soft)

From ... qualitative description (sheltered/exposed) ... to ... quantitative measurements (0 m/sec, 2m/sec, 4m/sec)

From ... simple equipment (gun clinometer) ... to ... complex equipment (abney level)

Analysis and Interpretation:

From ... pictographs, bar graphs ... to ... pie charts, scatter graphs

From ... describe sites as good or bad ... to ... rank sites in order

From ... analyse limited number of variables (slope, windiness) ... to ... analyse wide range of physical factors (slope, wind, wetness, warmth, ground hardness) and consider other influences

May and Cook (1993) illustrated **progression in enquiry** as follows:

1. Increasing independence	– in planning – in preparation – in execution – in evaluation	3. Increasing sophistication of technique in	– data gathering – data handling – interpretation – presentation
2. Increasing depth of study		4. Increasing rigour throughout	

Figure 2.7 Progression in fieldwork tasks

A commonly quoted example concerns the development of plan views where the progression is from elevation (front on views) to oblique aerial views to vertical aerial views. In direction, signpost maps can be developed in sequence from a desk top, to objects in the room, to objects in the school grounds, to objects on the horizon. With coordinates the progession is from alphanumeric grids with the letters representing the space between the grid lines, to two number coordinates between grids, to two number coordinates on the grid lines, to three figure references on the grid lines.

Progression in Places

Lawson and Schiavone (1995) identify the three broad lines of progression in the study of places: knowledge of the locations, character of the places and comparison of the places. For example, with the comparison of places at Step 1 the pupils are required to recognise differences and similarities between the local area and a contrasting area; at Step 2 they are required to make comparisons between the local area and other areas and offer some reasons for the similarities and differences; at Step 3 they compare areas by referring to a variety of physical and human features and describe and explain the reasons for the similarities and differences.

Section 4: Differentiation

Definitions

Tackling differentiation can really tax our skills as teachers! (Piggott, 1995).

Matching activities to individual pupils' abilities is a very demanding professional skill (CCW, 1991).

Turning a theoretical grasp of this issue into actual planning and teaching is very demanding (NCC, 1993).

Is differentiation really that difficult? Many teachers consider it so, especially with the current increases in class size. Four recent discussions of this subject (Piggott, 1995; Blyth and Krause, 1995; Foley and Janikoun, 1992; and NCC, 1993) have all made use of the same case study: perhaps good practice is difficult to come by.

Differentiation is the process in the organisation of learning that enables all children to learn effectively, to be given opportunities to show what they know, understand and can do in a positive way and can achieve their full potential (NCC, 1993).

Organisation in and beyond the classroom

Are pupils to be grouped to
– enable individual/group progress?
– assist motivation?

How do we ensure there is a close link between individuals or groups and differentiated materials?

Teacher intervention

How do we ensure that teacher questioning is stimulating and motivating for the individual or group?

Will the sophistication of language vary from group to group, individual to individual?

Resources

Are pupils being guided to appropriate resources in terms of their variety and complexity?

Is there varying detail on maps/diagrams/reading age of materials/variety of contexts?

In class support

To what extent should the class teacher/support teachers assist individuals/groups?

Have individual targets been set, and are tasks broken down into small achievable steps?

Will most pupils follow a common task, and the teacher make an opportunity for individual support?

Strategies for learning

Will the strategies enable all children to get started?

Is there scope for the less able children to demonstrate their ability levels?

Will there be opportunities for more able pupils to work at greater levels of abstraction, depth and breadth?

Figure 2.8 Questions to ask when planning for differentiation (Piggott 1993; 1995).

Children learn at different rates, in different ways and with different degrees of success. The curriculum must be differentiated in terms of the level of work, pace of teaching and language level and this should also be tailored to the different physical, sensory, emotional and social needs of the pupils. All pupils, including those with special needs and those who are gifted, should be progressively challenged by their learning in geography.

Differentiation involves:

1. Using a range of teaching and learning styles which can build on the interests and experiences of children, ie no one should be excluded.
2. Matching tasks to individual children's needs.
3. Linking planning, learning, teaching and assessment in a cycle to identify and match tasks to needs.
4. Recognising individual entitlement and access to the National Curriculum.
(NCC, 1993).

Piggott (1993; 1995) proposes a number of key questions (related to organisation, teacher intervention, resources, in class support and strategies for learning) to be asked when planning for differentiation (see Figure 2.8).

Forms of Differentiation

The NCC (1993) provides a widely quoted example to illustrate differentiation. The task is to observe the geographical features in the school grounds. The children are asked to observe the view in the school playground and to compare it with a prepared sketch of the same view (Figure 2.9). Children respond in different ways. One child might respond by:

1. Using the teacher's sketch to describe, in words, some of the features, eg the tarmac, playground and flower beds.
2. Pointing to these directly and on the sketch, requiring the teacher to record these observations.
3. Colouring in certain components to demonstrate knowledge of their position and extent, eg playground = grey; flower beds = brown.

Another child might respond by:

1. Taking the sketch and adding to it from direct observations.
2. Selecting, unaided, a range of important features.
3. Inventing and applying labels to these features.

In this example the teacher has set a *common task* and achieved differentiation by outcome. This is the first of five strategies for differentiation, all of which are used almost intuitively by many teachers. These are:

1. Common task.
2. Stepped task.
3. Separate tasks for separate groups.
4. Different resources, same task
5. Teacher support tailored to individual or group needs.

A second strategy, *stepped task*, involves progressively more demanding stages and an expectation that some children will cover only the early tasks. For example, all children are asked to start their work by colouring buildings and grass different colours. Four further steps may then follow sequentially: (i) identifying three named features; (ii) completing and adding to the sketch with their own labels; (iii) adding estimated distances and sizes to the sketch; and (iv) offering explanations for some of their observations.

A third strategy, *separate tasks for separate groups*, involves grouping the children according to ability or other criteria. A range of different tasks is set to meet the needs of each group. For example, one group may use the sketch and common tasks of strategy 1; a second group of children who are good at speaking but less so at writing and drawing, may use a tape recorder to interview people about the features observed; a third group of children, who are able to observe but unable to convert their observations into a sketch, might make a list of words or pictures to indicate the features. Here differentiation is by pupil grouping.

With the fourth strategy, *different resources, same task*, the least able children are given the full sketch with key labels in place, and the most able are given only an outline with

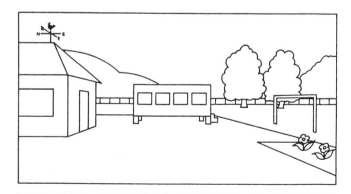

Figure 2.9 A sample task: observing geographical features in the school grounds (NCC, 1993).

no labels. The first requires the children to make additional labels and observations; the second requires greater analysis and imagination.

A fifth strategy is called *teacher support tailored to individual or group needs*. All children go into the school grounds with the same sketch and instructions. The teacher gives support to the weaker children using guided question and answer techniques. Different language levels can be used according to ability and those pupils with special educational needs can be given help with writing and reading.

A second example of planning for differentiation (also from the NCC, 1993) involves *Water on the Move*. Here there are two distinct groups of Year 6 children, one of mixed ability (including statemented children) and another with pupils of high ability. Differentiation is built into the planning through different objectives, children's tasks, resources and contexts. For the mixed ability group the objectives are broad, the tasks are capable of high and low level responses, the strategies are varied and the resources range from fieldwork equipment to aerial photographs.

Children in the most able group also follow the preceding core activities based on the parts of the river system, experimenting with the processes of erosion, transportation and deposition in sand trays. However the extension work is to prepare a booklet for a house for sale situated on the river bank experiencing erosion. The tasks are open, with little guidance being given. They require the accurate application of detailed knowledge about river erosion to a particular situation as well as reasoned, extended argument. Some of the resources are to be gathered by the children using their own contacts.

The example in the previous paragraph raises the issue of equal opportunities for children of different socioeconomic backgrounds. Some children are more able to obtain appropriate resources because of their home backgrounds: the teacher's responsibility is to ensure that children from less privileged backgrounds have equal access to learning resources.

May and Cook (1993) offer five ways of achieving differentiation within enquiry:

1. Through the questions posed.
2. Through the level of support given to pupils, the selection of resources, the amount and detail of pupil planning, and the scope of the enquiry.
3. Through different fieldwork tasks set with regard to content, scope, level and equipment used. →

4. Through collecting and collating tasks, and through presenting outcomes in terms of content and level of communication.
5. Through levels of attainment and methods of presentation in reporting and through the selection of the areas to be evaluated.

For those interested in how they rate on differentiation, the Supplementary Materials 5 will be of interest (Piggott, 1995).

Section 5: Assessment

There is no requirement to conduct end of key stage assessments in geography in 1996 or 1997. This means there is no statutory obligation for teachers to record and report children's attainments in the form of levels for the subject at the end of the key stage … The issue of statutory teacher assessment in Key Stages 1 and 2 in 1998 and thereafter is to be reviewed in 1995-6. … Teachers are however required to report progress in geography at the end of the key stage (SCAA, 1995).

In both Key Stages 1 and 2 the practices of assessment, recording and reporting caused difficulties. Work was marked and parents received reports, but assessment practices were often weak or non-existent: teachers tended to record what lessons had covered rather than what pupils had achieved. Reporting of progress to parents was generally satisfactory (OFSTED, 1995).

Purposes of Assessment

Testing children is a long established process and has traditionally been done for one of two purposes:

Summatively, to establish what a pupil knows, understands and can do, in order to evaluate the effectiveness of teaching and learning. Such assessment involves the comparison of a pupil's skills, knowledge and understanding against some external norms, such as the National Curriculum level descriptions. Results of summative assessment are important for a range of people, including the class teacher, head-teacher, governors, parents, other teachers, potential parents, OFSTED and the local newspaper. In this the teacher's role is analogous to the driving test examiner who either passes or fails the learner driver (Blyth and Krause, 1995).

Formatively, to help monitor achievement on a continuing basis in order to improve the teaching and learning process. At the heart of formative assessment is the process of feedback. Formative assessment is, in essence, a process by which the teacher's work is continuously influenced by the feedback obtained from assessment. Results are mainly of relevance to teachers and pupils. Here the analogy is with the driving instructor who identifies problems with the driver and takes steps to correct the faults.

However, more recently teacher assessment is being used

to serve bureaucratic purposes, such as the requirement that the education system, schools and individual teachers are accountable through some form of simple 'output' measure. This could possibly lead to assessment scores being published in the form of league tables (Butt et al, 1995).

Uses of Assessment

Assessment is useful for:

1. Providing information about teaching and learning in geography.
2. Helping teachers plan future teaching and learning activities, and evaluating them.
3. Detecting and diagnosing difficulties experienced by individual pupils.
4. Informing pupils and parents on progress.

Good assessment requires a diversity of techniques, tasks and learning strategies so that pupils are given a variety of ways in which to demonstrate their achievement

(see Figure 2.11, from Foley and Janikoun, 1992). Figure 2.10 illustrates an approach to the assessment of *weather* in Key Stages 1 and 2 between levels 1 and 5.

The single NC geography attainment target emphasises the integration of the subject and simplifies assessment, recording and reporting procedures (Ranger, 1995). Level descriptions (LDs) have replaced the earlier statements of attainment. The essential function of LDs is to assist in making summative judgements about pupils' performance at the end of Key Stage 2. They indicate the types and range of performance which pupils working at a particular level should characteristically demonstrate. Teachers are required to exercise professional judgement in establishing the 'best-fit' between the pupil's performance and the appropriate level description. The aim of teacher assessment should be to arrive at an all-round judgement of the level the pupil has achieved on the basis of evidence collected from a number of sources over time.

Evidence for Assessment

Evidence of pupil achievement can be derived from a range of sources:

1. Observations of pupils at work, individually or in groups.
2. Responses made by children to the teacher's questions.
3. Written work.
4. Results of tests.

Assessment Method			
Level 1	Discussion with individual children.	**Level 4**	Observe weather using rain gauge and thermometer for 1 week and present results accurately in tabular form.
Level 2	Draw pictures to illustrate different weather conditions.		
	Examine photographs of four seasons and correctly label.		Devise a board game to show the relationship between the weather extremities in other parts of the world and its effect on human beings.
Level 3	Identify, by placing under the correct headings, photographs depicting equatorial, polar, hot desert and temperate regions.	**Level 5**	Design an enquiry into choosing the site for a washing line. Choose parameters which are to be measured and the equipment and skills required.
	Make own postcards from different climatic zones to show which climatic zone they are in giving at least three clues.		Collect the daily weather information from a contrasting foreign locality, store in a database and compare with the data collected in the home area.

Figure 2.10 An approach to the assessment of weather

Type of activity		Geographical context
OS map	Using and interpreting maps	Story to include features you can see from a given grid reference. Postcards: stand at point X and draw what you can see. Swap cards with other pupils – where was your postcard written? Give a detailed account of a journey from points A to B by car or foot. Signpost maps from given grid references.
Atlas	Make your own postcard	Postcards to show which country you are in. Give at least three clues in your picture and writing.
Map and plan	Giving directions to other children	Can they follow instructions? Where did they end up? Construct maps for younger children. Do they need a key? How much information to put in?
	Listen to instructions	Draw a map of X's route to school.
	Types of maps	What sort of map would you need to ...? Who would use ... type of map?
Factual recall	Normal classroom writing	Write two pieces of work, one before and one after about a place/issue. Make up a crossword or word search to include some clues and facts on a given topic. Devise a test for your friends and construct an answer sheet.
Vocabulary	Explanations of vocabulary and concepts	Write a sentence/paragraph/draw a picture to illustrate x. Geographical cloze procedure with or without words. Use the following geographical terms correctly, hill, reservoir, etc
Drama	Role play and/or assemblies	If possible these should be written by the children, eg a day in the life of a family in India.
Tape	Tape recording of discussion or explanation	Explain settlement types from pictures.
Artwork	'Before and after' pictures	Draw in different mediums, eg mountains and rock strata or deserts.
Treasure trails	Directional competitions	Design a trail. Follow a trail.
	Orienteering	Collect letters to make up a word.
Playground games	Directional games	Bounce ball on a large map of unnamed countries. Move to N, S, E, W.
Board games	Designed by the children	Cross curricular games (geography, technology, maths, English): routes, treasure islands, collecting sets of different shop types, etc.
Computer	Directional activities	Logo for spatial awareness. Roamers and Turtles can all be used to check direction and routes.
	Databases	Use atlas, book to fill gaps in a database. Add climate statistics or place names.
Technology	Project briefs	Include geography, grid references taught previously, eg playground, park or room plans.
Poems	Write a poem	Follow a route on a map or draw a map to go with a written poem.
Video	Video and discussion	For teacher moderation and consideration: pupils make video about an issue, eg siting a new local pub, supermarket or park.
Photographs	Take or use them	Where were these taken on the trail? Can you map them, identify them or take them at given points? Spot trails are adaptable to age levels. Sort and locate photographic evidence.

Figure 2.11 Opportunities for teacher assessment in primary geography (Foley and Janikoun, 1992).

Graphical evidence	Written evidence	Oral evidence
Maps Drawings Diagrams Graphs Print-out Photographs	Reports Notes Diaries Questionnaires Stories Essays Newspaper articles Short answer questions Multiple choice questions Cloze procedure	Questioning Discussion Interviews Sequencing Role play Pupil presentations Tapes Video recordings Debates
Products		
Models Artefacts		

Figure 2.12 Types of assessment evidence.

Informal evidence available to the teacher consists of observations, photographs, records and notes. Evidence also comes in numerous forms whether it be written (eg a report of a freak period of weather), graphical (eg a bar graph showing the amount of rain during the storm), oral (eg a tape recording of the child interviewing an older person affected by the storm) or a product (eg a model of a rain god made by the pupil) – see Figure 2.11.

Level Descriptions

By the end of Key Stage 2 most pupils will be within the range of levels 2 to 5. It is necessary for teachers to record what has been taught and to assess how far individual pupils have progressed in knowledge, understanding and skills. Level descriptions do not replace the ongoing, formative, teacher assessment that is essential for good teaching.

The level descriptions have been written to represent progression in terms of the five facets examined in the following five paragraphs. Progression occurs in terms of:

(i) Pupils' ability to show their knowledge, understanding and skills in studies at a widening range of scales and in contrasting contexts. Examples are the concentric movement from the local to the global and from the study of a locality in an advanced, temperate, industrial nation to one in a less developed, agricultural, tropical country.

(ii) Pupils' ability to draw on a widening range of geographical skills and use them with increasing selectivity, accuracy and independence. An example is the increased use of progressively more complicated equipment to record the weather.

(iii) A growing understanding of the similarities and differences between places. An example is the increase in sophistication in awareness of place differences, from obvious ones associated with climate and landforms (eg UK compared with a mountainous desert) to more subtle differences associated with culture, political organisation and economic development.

(iv) A growing understanding of human and physical processes in geography and the effects of their interactions. An example is the progression in understanding of *migration* from one represented as "my auntie lives in Australia" to one expressed as "she moved because there were no jobs at home and Australia wanted to increase its population".

(v) A growing understanding about the ways in which environmental issues arise and are tackled, eg progression from an awareness that desertification in Africa is caused by lack of rain and can be solved by sending out food, to an awareness that there may be other causes associated with population levels and over use of the land and that merely sending out bags of food will relieve the problem for a short time but not solve it.

Section 6: Teaching and Learning Strategies

One of the great contributions of geography to the Key Stage 2 curriculum arises from its ability to provide a wide range of teaching and learning strategies. As a result, geography brings variety to the classroom and allows teachers to focus particular methods on selected pupils. This has obvious implications for motivation and improved learning.

Teaching strategy refers to the broad approach or package of methods and techniques employed by the teacher to foster learning. Once the strategy has been identified, the teacher stimulates children's learning through a very wide range of more detailed 'tactics' which are concerned with classroom management and which are beyond the scope of this book. *Teaching style* refers to something different from strategy. It is the outcome of the teacher's approach to relationships, values and behavioural norms which she/he chooses to foster. The most common terms are 'formal' and 'informal'. 'Style' is independent of strategy: for example, a teacher can use IT or an outside visitor in an informal or in a formal way.

The range of strategies available to the teacher of geography is large and includes:

1. Fieldwork.
2. Creative activities.
3. Questions and answers.
4. Individual and group enquiries.
5. Use of photographs, television, radio, tape, video and film.
6. Use of IT.
7. Use of books, leaflets, maps, atlases, newspapers.
8. Role play and drama.
9. Simulations.
10. Use of visitors and outside speakers.

A powerful influence on teaching strategy is the philosophical stance of the teacher, especially with regard to the development of children's autonomy and independence. The key element in this is the teacher-centred to child-centred continuum. At one end of the scale the teacher provides teacher chosen curriculum content (often information) which the children merely receive. At the other end the teacher provides support for learning through resources, equipment and location whilst the children are fully responsible for the choice of activity, be it creative drama, discovery learning, project-based or whatever (see Figure 2.13).

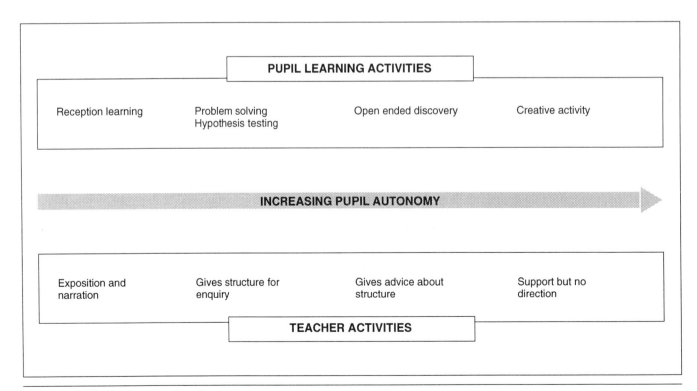

Figure 2.13 The development of pupil autonomy.

The development of pupil autonomy implicit in the geography curriculum is apparent from the following two sets of quotes from the level descriptions.

Resources: Children should:

1. *Use resources provided (level 1).*
2. *Select information from resources provided (level 2).*
3. *Select and use (level 5).*
4. *Select and make effective use (level 6).*

Questions: Children should:

1. *Respond to questions (level 1).*
2. *Ask and respond to questions (level 2).*
3. *Use skills and sources of evidence to respond to a range of geographical questions (level 3).*
4. *Draw on their knowledge and understanding to suggest suitable geographical questions (level 4).*
5. *Identify relevant questions (level 5).*
6. *Identify relevant geographical questions and suggest appropriate sequences of investigation (level 6).*

Teaching and Learning Styles in Fieldwork

Booth et al (1993) identified 32 terms to describe fieldwork, ranging from 'The Cook's Tour' through 'talk and gawk' to hypothesis testing and problem solving (see Figure 2.14).

Opportunities in geography ... and maths, art, technology, English, science ...

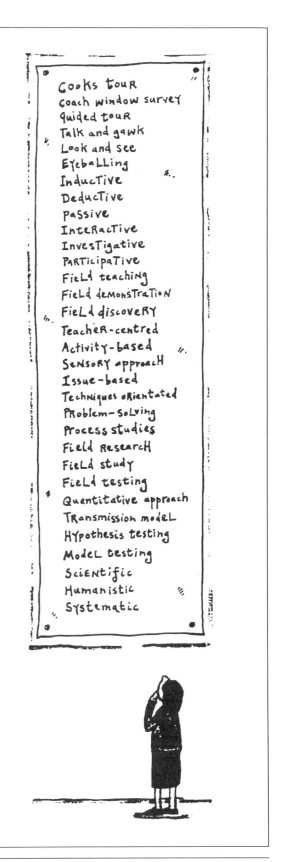

Figure 2.14 Fieldwork: How shall we do it today? Source: Booth, R. Chambers, W. J. and Thomas, A. D. (1993) Reaching Out. London, Living Earth/ICI

The approach chosen will reflect the following:

1. The knowledge, intuition and experience of the teacher.
2. The nature, commitment, personality and experience of the pupils.
3. The demands of the National Curriculum.
4. The nature of the fieldwork location.
5. The aims and balance of the fieldwork.
6. The educational philosophy of the individual teacher and the school.

As with most aspects of the curriculum, variety of approach is to be preferred.

From the wide range of fieldwork strategies, three main approaches are commonly used, *look and see*, the *investigative* and the *enquiry-based*. The characteristics of each of these is shown in Figure 2.16.

Each of these is now described, using *a street* as an example. (see Figure 2.15).

Street Fieldwork

Look and See: teacher has the knowledge

Process: Show, observe, listen, draw, photograph, demonstrate, guided tour, follow trail, meet the Mayor, the planner

Teacher says: In 1863 … Can you see … There are 3 possible … Ms Snape will tell you … Answer the worksheet …

Pupils say: Can you repeat that?… I can't hear..... What do you want us to do?..... I've never noticed that before …

Themes: Old and new ... Continuity and change … Building function … Land use … Conservation areas … Transport.

Investigative: teacher provides the equipment and topic

Process: Measure, count, survey, sample, sense, questionnaire

Teacher says: Imagine you're a real researcher ...To find this out you will need … Make sure you've got enough information … Are there any trends or patterns?

Pupils say: So that's how it's done … How many shall we interview? … Where shall we? … How often …?

Themes: Relationship between size of road and volume and type of traffic using traffic counts … Number of customers and type of shop using pedestrian census … Environmental quality using streetometer.

Enquiry: teacher provides sources of information and resources

Process: Discovery … guided discovery … enquiry … role play … issue-based … purposeful data collection

Teacher says: What do you think? … How could we …? What view does each group take? … The Planners say … Why doesn't anyone …?

Pupils say: There's no easy solution.... I've looked at all the evidence and … Our results could be used by … Now I know what it feels like …

Themes: Locating a new zebra crossing... Using the waste ground on the corner … Pedestrianising the High Street … Allowing disabled access.

Figure 2.15 An example of a range of fieldwork strategies

Fieldwork activities	Look and See "Out of the window you can see ..."	Investigative "If it moves, measure it"	Enquiry "There's no simple answer"
Type of activity	eye-balling Cooks tour talk and gawk guided tour field teaching	field study field testing investigating process studies model testing pure	field discovery hypothesis testing issues problem solving applied
Characteristics	passive transmission teacher-centred factual knowledge prescriptive specific qualitative observation-orientated non-participatory information-based	active finding out teacher led, pupil centred methodological systematic scientific qualitative and quantitative measurement-orientated participatory activity-based	interactive evaluating pupil centred, pupil led interpretative open ended scientific and humanistic qualitative and quantitative outcome-orientated fully participatory discovery-based

Figure 2.16 Three types of fieldwork activity.

Habitats provide opportunities for work in environmental education, a cross curricular theme.

Section 7: Resources

... the truth is that the best resource is a sensitive teacher (Brough, 1983).

Despite Brough's comment, it takes a unique teacher with limitless knowledge, creativity and energy to teach a geography curriculum without using supplementary resources. Indeed, with the distant locality requirements and the wide availability of magnificent videos and colour photographs, it would be arrogant in the extreme to assume that any one teacher could (without the help of significant resources) deliver the National Curriculum geography at Key Stage 2!

OFSTED's experience has been uneven. In their report of their 1993/4 inspection findings they found that:

the resourcing of geography (at Key Stages 1 and 2) ... ranged from very good to poor. Some schools had made considerable investments in atlases, maps, photographs and reference books and used them well. In others, resources were inappropriate or non-existent, and at times the poor storage of resources restricted their use.

Types of Resource

As an indication of the wide range of resources which are appropriate for Key Stage 2 geography, it is possible to list over 90, ranging from activity cards to workbooks (see Figure 2.17).

An unfinished checklist of resources*		
activity cards	guest speakers	questionnaires
archives	interviews	radio
artefacts	item banks	readings
audio tapes	jigsaw puzzle maps	recipes
brochures	journals	recordings
bulletin boards	letters	reports
cartoons	line sketches	reproductions
case studies	logs	research findings
cassettes	magazines	role plays
census findings	maps	sand tables
chalkboard	mobiles	scrapbooks
charts	mock ups	simulations
collages	mock newscasts	slides
collections	making models	sociodrama
computer-assisted	montages	specimens
learning packages	murals	stamps
cross sections	music	statistics
crossword puzzles	narratives	stencils
diaries	newsletters	stories
dioramas	newspapers	surveys
documents	novels	tables
excursions	overhead projector	talks
exhibits	transparencies	tape recordings
fieldstudies	paintings	television
films	pamphlets	tests
filmstrips	parents	textbooks
flags	pen pals	timelines
flannelboards	people	touring guides
flashcards	periodicals	transparencies
flowcharts	photographs	trips
games	pictures	video
globes	poetry	workbooks ...
graphs	posters	

* Although many of these might be viewed as activities, the results of these activities can provide valuable resources for other students

Figure 2.17 Resources available to geography teachers. Source: MacColl P (1984) in Fien J et al (1984)

There are many ways to classify resources. Hindson (1989) uses the following categories in his discussion of secondary school geography departments. Readers may wish to attempt a similar classification for their own schools:

1. People – teachers, including the curriculum co-ordinator and the wide range of skills and interests possessed by other teachers as a result of their leisure activities; other school staff, parents, regular visitors and invited guests.
2. Fixed – accommodation (the classroom and its fittings).
3. Fixed – storage space (a geography store cupboard, room or base).
4. Fixed – other rooms containing geographical resources, such as libraries, the IT and science rooms.
5. Moveable – by far the largest group, including books, packs and videos.

In addition we can add the following fixed resources: the school grounds and local environment, local libraries, museums, galleries, industries, educational venues and the local authority field studies centre (Booth et al, 1993).

Foley and Janikoun (1992) classified their list of (moveable) resources as follows:

1. Text books and schemes.
2. Atlases.
3. Maps and plans.
4. Globes.
5. Other equipment (compasses, clinometers, and weather measuring equipment).
6. Vertical aerial photographs.
7. Information technology.
8. Media and audio visual aids.
9. Useful addresses for UK studies.
10. Useful addresses for distant places studies.
11. Packs.
12. The Geographical Association.
13. Teacher's books.
14. HMI publications.
15. Magazines.
16. Story books.

This forms a comprehensive *aide-memoire* for the geography or humanities coordinator when considering the full range of resources potentially available to the school.

Within the last category many writers such as Bowles (1993) and Palmer (1994) have published comprehensive lists, whilst Foley and Janikoun (1992) have included a classified and detailed list of resources in their textbook. At a more reflective level, Blyth and Krause (1995) have excellent guidelines on *Choosing and Using Resources*. In addition, newspapers and journals such as *The Times Educational Supplement* and *Primary Geographer* have regular reviews and the latter has produced a review of atlases and locality packs. The best place to see geography resources is the Annual Conference of the Geographical Association held at Easter.

In 1992 Jo Hughes attempted to identify and price the resources needed to "get primary geography going". Her total came to £2651 which included £1100 for a computer, Roamer, concept keyboard, printer and tape recorders. In addition £84 was allowed for weather measuring equipment which may be jointly purchased from the science budget.

Resourcing Parts of the Geography Curriculum

Various people have produced their own checklist of resources for geography. Catling (1990) produced a list of 38 different types of map (see Figure 2.18), the vast majority being free. Fundamental to any Key Stage 2 curriculum is a large scale map of the local environment at a scale of 1:1 250, a set of atlases and a globe. Closely associated with the maps are vertical and oblique aerial photographs at a large scale, some at the same scale and covering the same area as the large scale maps.

To help a teacher resource a study of the local area there are numerous lists. Most obvious are the existing physical, environmental and human resources such as the river, hill, park, bus station, motorway, block of flats and chip shop. The Curriculum Council for Wales (1992) identified the following:

1. Maps.
2. Questionnaires.
3. Photographs.
4. Newspaper cuttings.
5. Weather records.
6. Slides.
7. Tape recordings of interviews.
8. Estate agents' advertisements.
9. Statistics.
10. Outline maps.
11. Census data.
12. Kelly's directories.
13. Geological samples. →

14. Videos.
15. Contact names in local businesses.
16. Tourist information.

At the scale of the distant locality, most learning will be second-hand (Hughes and Marsden, 1994). One criterion for choice of locality may well be availability of resources. The National Curriculum geography Order has stimulated

---

Maps

street maps	building plans
postcard maps	road maps
maps in adverts	road sign maps
housing estate maps	town centre maps
tourist area maps	trail maps
Ordnance Survey maps	bus route maps
railway maps	underground maps
room plans	storybook maps
board game maps	maps on stamps
textbook maps	atlas maps
wallchart maps	guidebook maps
maps drawn by children	teacher drawn maps
maps in birthday cards	picture maps
landuse maps	'antique' maps
resort maps	sketch maps
playmat maps	newspaper maps
maps on mugs	tea-towel maps
building site plans	globes
teaching pack maps	computer software maps

Figure 2.18 The variety of maps to collect. Source: Catling (1990).

St Lucia Rich Resources?

Activity pack (GA)

28 colour photographs
Harvey family at home, school, church
Growing up in Castries: Hayle Harvey
Urban, rural and banana landscapes

Primary Geographer **St Lucia Special Issue, Spring 1992**

The Harvey Family
The Anglican Infant School
Getting Around St Lucia (travel & journeys)
Landscapes and Weather, Volcanoes and Hurricanes
Photographs
How an Island Earns its Living (work, land use and settlement)
Land of Beaches (the sea as a resource)
Resources, Environment and Development (urban, rural, industrial, agricultural)

Primary Geographer **St Lucia Special, July 1995**

Harvey family update
Anglican Infant School update
Planning a visit to St Lucia
Settlement in St Lucia
St Lucia Fact File
St Lucia (Simply Beautiful) song
A trip to Castries (make-believe)
Maggie Mouse goes Adventuring (story, environment)
Environmental Change in St Lucia (and issues)
Satellite map poster (Worldaware)
Environmental Choices Game
A sense of St Lucia (poem)
Plan of a St Lucia study unit
Geography in Children's books
Geography through Stamps
Devastating Debbie
Scenes from Castries (photographs)

Images of Earth: a teacher's guide to remote sensing at key stage 2 (GA)

Distant Places CD-ROM (Advisory Unit for Computers in Education)

Ordnance Survey Worldmap 4: St Lucia

St Lucia Mapcard

**TV: BBC: 10 programmes;
Channel 4: Geography – Start Here? Penpals**

Slide sets (Worldaware): bananas; the Harvey family home; transport and links

20 Lessons on St Lucia

Figure 2.19 Resourcing parts of the geography curriculum.

the publication of numerous resources on the same locality, thus extending the resources available to schools for study of a distant locality. A good example is St Lucia in the West Indies. Wendy Morgan (1992) has recommended the following essential resources to support distant locality studies:

1. Firsthand study (ie a visit!).
2. Second-hand experience from the class teacher or a visitor (native or foreigner).
3. Photographs.
4. Maps.
5. Pictures.
6. Slides.
7. Film or video.
8. Oblique aerial photographs.
9. Vertical aerial photographs.
10. Written descriptions.
11. Statistical data about weather and jobs.

In addition she lists a number of desirable resources:

1. Somebody who has visited the locality.
2. Audio tapes or radio programme about the locality.
3. First hand written or audio accounts from local people.
4. Published materials which support learning activities.
5. Satellite images.
6. Songs and music, local art and craft work.
7. Pupils' games.
8. A range of artefacts indicative of lifestyle.

Other useful resources include postal or electronic links with a local school, story books about the place, diaries of the children and postcards.

Resource Strategies

In recent years it has been difficult to establish and maintain a consistent resource strategy. Both schools and publishers have been reluctant to commit themselves to the purchase and production of resources, given the curricular instability. Resource production and purchase have focused on the core subjects of mathematics, science and English. With the moratorium on further major curriculum change until the year 2000 it is now possible to think seriously about the systematic and planned purchase of resources.

A significant professional responsibility of the geography/humanities coordinator is to convince the headteacher that geography should have access to appropriate resources. Another priority is to ensure that the amount allocated is adequate for the needs of the children. It is also necessary to devise a system for the allocation of the capitation: will it be done on a year by year or a class by class approach or will individual units of study be resourced on a rotating basis? Which resources will be single copies and which class sets? If single copies are purchased with photocopiable masters how is the photocopying going to be funded? Can resources be shared between different budget heads? For example, can reference atlases be funded from library allocation, weather instruments from science funds, tape measures and compasses from mathematics? Can geography have access to Parent Teacher Association funds? What happens to grant money for landscape improvements or other environmental projects?

Evaluating Resources

Marsden presented the following guidelines for evaluating published materials on a GEST course for Cheshire teachers.

1. Good geographical practice

- *Do the materials provide opportunities for the development of a wide range of geographical skills, knowledge and understanding of the places, themes and environmental change specified in the National Curriculum?*

- *Are the materials geographically correct, with accurate and up to date information?*

2. Good primary practice

- *Do the materials encourage enquiry?*

- *Do they offer opportunities for differentiation?*

- *Are the activities, where relevant, open ended with clear and challenging extension tasks?*

- *Are the materials interesting?*

- *Do they allow the children to show progression in their learning?*

3. Values and attitudes

- *Do the materials avoid stereotyping?*

- *Do they provide equality of opportunity?*

- *Do they show other people, their culture and environment in a sensitive, non-stereotypical manner?*

- *Do the materials encourage the children to reflect on their own value positions and develop responsible attitudes?*

Children's skills in observation, sorting and recording can be developed through the use of some basic resources.

The Nitty Gritty of Resources

The first step in organising and managing resources is to audit existing materials and discard those materials which are out of date or do not satisfy the teacher's chosen criteria, or those proposed by Marsden, above. Many teachers find this difficult!

The next step is to identify the shortcomings in current resourcing and then prioritise needs. The financial allocation to geography must be discussed and agreed with the headteacher.

Free resources are produced by a large number of commercial organisations. It is important to ensure that bias is kept to a minimum, given that most producers of free and glossy materials do so for promotional rather than purely educational reasons. The issues are complex. Many such materials are prepared by practising teachers, often on secondment to the company. They may be given a brief to produce high quality learning materials on a given topic. The class teacher has the responsibility to bring to bear professional judgement when it comes to bias and underlying motives of the producing company.

Resource boxes, files or databases on key National Curriculum geography themes, topics or localities should be built up. Key stage planning plus the maintenance of units of work within topics for several cycles of learning make for stability and, therefore, more effective use of teacher time.

The storage and access of learning materials are crucial and often seen as straightforward. They are not. As Hindson (1989) says, "a chaotic stock cupboard should be regarded not as a charming eccentricity, but as industrial sabotage – wasting, for all who have to grapple with it, the precious resources of time and patience". A central school resource area is often economic of space, cheaper and easier to monitor than several smaller ones and allows teachers cross curricular browsing.

The alternative approach, of individual class storage, assumes that all units of work are limited to one class at any one time. For schools using two year rotation systems it assumes that it is always possible to distinguish between, say, Year 3 and Year 5 materials on the same topic. It gives maximum convenience to individual class teachers but maximum inconvenience for others. A compromise based on the central storage of high value (eg computer software), high bulk (eg globes) or high frequency of use items (eg maps and aerial photographs of the school locality) and classroom storage of topic-specific items is probably a satisfactory compromise.

Chapter 3: The Role of Information Technology in Geography at Key Stage 2

Section 1: The Role of IT

The Dearing Report (1993) recommended that 36 hours a year should be used to develop children's IT (Information Technology) skills through other subjects at Key Stage 2. This chapter suggests some elements of classroom capability in geography, with particular reference to practical examples and recent developments, including the use of CD-ROM, satellite imagery and electronic communication. Fitting IT into the Key Stage 2 curriculum poses many challenges for teachers, but with the focus on geography these can readily be overcome with suitable resource planning and management.

There was a time when Information Technology (IT) may have struck fear into the hearts of even the most experienced and adventurous teachers. But this is not the case today, largely because IT has become very user friendly and computers have become a part of everyday life. There are many different sides to IT and therefore many types of approach, suitable for all classroom practitioners.

Teaching and Learning

IT can help pupils to learn geography in many ways and most of these are very easy for the Key Stage 2 teacher to organise and manage. There are many familiar issues associated with teaching and learning with IT. These include:

1. Encouraging and enhancing enquiry-based learning.
2. Providing a range of information sources to enhance teaching and learning in geography.
3. Supporting the development of pupils' understanding of geographical patterns and processes.
4. Providing access to images of people, places and environments which might otherwise not be readily available.
5. Contributing to the pupils' awareness of the impact of IT on the world about them.

How has IT been used to achieve these ends? Examples which illustrate the contribution that IT can make to children's learning in geography include a range of different types of software. These have been classified by topic and attainment target (Bowden 1992, see Figure 3.1). Topics include specific geographical skills such as maps and co-ordinates using programs such as *Map Venture* and applications which are content free such as wordprocessing, spreadsheets and databases. Bowden's classification by National Curriculum geography's earlier attainment targets include the use of geographical databases to investigate data for countries in the World, using for example *Development Data Search* or *World Map Study*, particularly in teaching distant locations, as described by Chambers (1992).

Classification by topic

Topics	Software
multi topic	No 62 Honeypot Lane
word and letter skills	Mystery Island
number skills	King of the Jungle
simulations and adventures	Pirate
geography and the environment	Around the World
wordprocessing and DTP	Caxton Press
databases, spreadsheets	Grass
maps and coordinates	Map Venture

Classification by theme

Theme	Software
geographical skills	Globe Trotter Plus
places	World Atlas 2.0
physical geography	Weather Report
human geography	Places and People
environment	Antarctica (Key)

Figure 3.1 Some software classifications. Source: adapted from Bowden D (1992).

Tools for IT: Hardware and Software

Computer hardware (the computer, keyboard, screen and mouse) usually belongs to one of four main types: BBC/Archimedes; Research Machines/Nimbus; Apple Macintosh; or IBM compatible (often labelled PC). Schools tend to stick to the same type of computer, although there is a strong argument in favour of diversity. Besides, systems are rapidly converging so the question of which platform is becoming redundant. Existing resources can normally still be used on the newer machines, though this is not always the case. For example, *Windows 95* on the PC requires updated versions of most standard wordprocessing and spreadsheet packages for efficient performance. Computers also rely on having extras (peripherals) such as printers, CD-ROM drives and dataloggers which need to be compatible.

Children's cognitive needs are crucial when devising a strategy for IT, although the software available is a constraint in some curriculum areas. The variety of programs is rapidly growing in number with many being reviewed or described in journals such as *Primary Geographer*. Further advice is available from many local education authorities, such as Lincolnshire, which recommends a geography and IT strategy (Eades and Weldon, 1995) and contains a wide variety of different IT applications (see Figure 3.2).

Types of software	Use in geography
Databases	to analyse data and produce graphs and data analysis
Spreadsheets	to input and present text and data, produce graphs and tables of information
Simulation programs	simulate real World situations, processes and patterns
Authoring (adventure software)	exploration, often dealing with geographical skills
Drill and practice	providing information and revision of ideas
Wordprocessing	production and presentation of text-based materials
Graphics	production of pictures, drawings and maps

Figure 3.2 Using types of computer software in geography.

Computer software has been classified on a number of bases (Bowden, 1992). However, there are generally two main types of software:

(i) Geography-specific software, which is subject-oriented and often skills-based eg *Map Venture* for learning about contours, or topic-based eg a simulation of nomadic herdsmen in *Sand Harvest* or migrants in *Developing Cities*.

(ii) Generic software, which is general software with applications in many subjects, such as wordprocessing or newspaper simulations eg *My World* and *Front Page*

Extra, or clip art to produce maps, drawings and displays or spreadsheets eg *Excel* or *Junior Pinpoint*.

The use of software in geography can be very varied and Bowden (1991) examines progression in teachers' use of software. At first, the software tends to be of limited educational value. The emphasis is on teachers' increasing confidence in IT. Teachers then progress in their use of software as they develop increasing experience and confidence. Eventually, Bowden suggests, a stage of unlimited teaching value is reached.

Until recently, very specific, content bound packages have tended to be more limited in value than the more open-ended, content free software. Thus, in order to enhance fully geography learning, you should include both subject specific and generic software across a wide range of skills areas and geographical themes.

Many valuable resources have been produced to deal with specific aspects of geography. An increasingly used resource in primary schools is the concept keyboard, with overlays on topics such as identification and classification keys. The concept keyboard replaces the normal computer keyboard and consists of an A4 or A3 sized block which is touch sensitive. It is connected to the computer which is programmed (easily, by the teacher) to display selected words or images whenever a given part of the concept keyboard is touched. Overlays are prepared according to specific needs.

Computer resources have been further enhanced by the development of CD-based technologies and these are considered in Section Five. A CD-ROM (Compact Disc-Read Only Memory) is a small disc which can contain large amounts of information including pictures, animation, sound and text. The two key attributes of CD-ROMS are (i) they hold huge amounts of data and (ii) the data can be quickly accessed. They provide substantial factual, visual and aural information which can be interrogated, searched, selected, edited, merged, saved to floppy disc and printed out. This enables pupils to investigate and discover subject-based information in an open ended context.

Some Applications

Information technology has many potential applications in the teaching and learning of geography, but they have not yet been taken up by teachers on a wide scale. OFSTED (1995) commented that the use of IT in geography was beginning to have a stimulating impact on a few schools through software, especially through geographical (ie content-specific) software. However, there is now a statutory requirement to include a significant element of IT in teaching and learning geography. "Pupils should be taught to use IT to gain access to additional information sources and to assist in handling, classifying and presenting evidence" (DFE, 1995a). In order to achieve this, Key Stage 2 teachers need to appreciate the opportunities which are available. The geography NC document suggests CD-ROM, wordprocessing and mapping software as possibilities. Davidson and Rudd (1993) identify three challenges for teachers of geography in their provision of IT experiences for children. These are to:

1. Provide opportunities for IT.
2. Successfully deliver and manage IT in the geography classroom.
3. Contribute to IT opportunities across the curriculum.

Integrating IT

Many recent developments have been concerned with helping teachers to integrate IT into their geography work. These include national initiatives, such as the Department for Education (DFE) *Computers in Primary Schools Initiative* and the subject initiative on *IT Entitlement Through Geography in 1996*, published by the Geographical Association as part of an update on developments in geography. In addition to such national initiatives, teachers can use a range of learning packs, such as *Learning Geography with Computers* (NCET, 1988) and in-service training resources like *Images of the Earth: A Teacher's Guide to Remote Sensing in Geography at Key Stage 2* (Barnett, Kent and Milton, 1995).

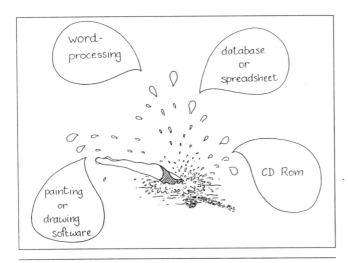

Figure 3.3 Taking the plunge: four simple ideas to get you using IT in geography at Key Stage 2.

In order to make effective use of IT in the classroom it is important for teachers to be aware of statutory requirements and thus be able to identify clear aims, before detailed planning and classroom practice can be implemented. Four ideas to get you started are provided in Figure 3.3.

Section 2: So What Is an IT Capability in Geography?

The Dearing Final Report (1993) indicated that the basics of information technology should be regarded as a core skill and that IT should be seen as an integral part of good practice in each subject. The geography programme of study states that: "Pupils should be given opportunities, where appropriate, to develop and apply information technology (IT) in their study of geography" (DFE, 1995a).

Entitlement to IT

Entitlement implies a statutory requirement whereby pupils should expect to gain competence during their school geography. The importance of entitlement is further reinforced by advice given by professional associations such as the Geographical Association and the National Council for Educational Technology (NCET) who both believe strongly in the importance of IT in the successful delivery of the geography curriculum. So what does IT have to offer children's learning in geography?

What is an IT Contribution?

The National Curriculum Order for information technology states that:

Information technology capability is characterised by an ability to use effectively IT tools and information sources to analyse, process and present information and to model, measure and control external events. This involves:

1. *Using information sources and IT tools to solve problems.*
2. *Using IT tools and information sources such as computer systems and software packages to support learning in a variety of contexts.*
3. *Understanding the implications of IT for working life and society.*

(DFE, 1995b).

The Geography and IT Support Project (1995) suggests five main areas where IT might contribute to a pupil's entitlement in geography:

1. Enhancing geographical enquiry.
2. Using a range of information sources to improve knowledge.
3. Understanding geographical patterns and processes.
4. Experiencing images of people, places and environments.
5. Increasing awareness of the impact of IT on the changing world.

There are many examples available which allow these aims to be achieved (see Figure 3.4). However, teachers frequently ask what IT can do for their own teaching (see Figure 3.5). Increasingly, children are able to take IT and the use of computers in their stride, readily adapting it to the classroom. The use of computers increases interest and motivation, opening many possibilities for investigating areas which might otherwise not be easily accessible.

Pupils studying geography can use IT to:	Possible example in Key Stage 2
enhance investigation and enquiry skills	investigate patterns and types of traffic flow using a spreadsheet
gain access to a wide range of geographical knowledge and information sources	use the Internet to access information from a wide range of sources around the World
deepen understanding of environmental and spatial relationships	present fieldwork data using computer generated graphs and wordprocessed text
experience alternative images of people, places and environment	use multimedia CD-ROM to find and collect information about distant places, the people and their cultures
consider the wider impact of IT on people, places and environment	consider how useful IT has become in school, the effect of new technology on the location of activities

Figure 3.4 Some uses of IT in geography at key stage 2.

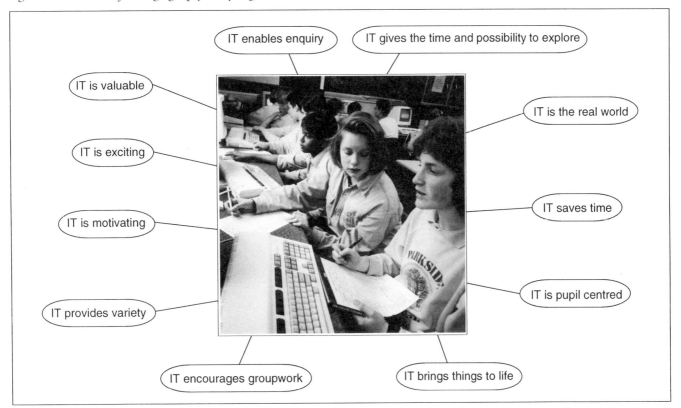

Figure 3.5 But what can IT do for you?

IT Strands

For curriculum purposes, information technology is represented as four strands (SCAA, 1995):

1. Communicating and handling information.
2. Controlling.
3. Modelling.
4. Monitoring.

This structure allows teachers to consider the learning opportunities of particular IT activities across the curriculum. Geography offers many valuable contexts where these strands might be delivered (see Figure 3.6).

Communicating and Handling Information

There are many ways in which children's IT skills in *communicating and handling information* can be developed in the context of geography. For example, the widely used content free (generic) software such as wordprocessing, desktop publishing, graphics packages and databases can be used to present the results of an enquiry or any piece of study. The software which allows children to present their findings in newspaper format is particularly easy to use and is most effective. Data handling is concerned with the storage, retrieval, modification and presentation of data. Children can thus explore patterns and relationships using the graphing and mapping functions of databases and spreadsheets. An example of this is illustrated by Harwood (1992), who describes how a spreadsheet can be used to analyse information collected about locations in the classroom. The children produce summaries in the form of averages, data tables and graphs using the spreadsheet

Grasshopper, leading to the analysis and interpretation of their results. Clearly, the opportunities for enquiry-based, cross curricular work are infinite and perhaps limited mainly by the teacher's imagination rather than by the constraints of modern software.

All generic software provides opportunities for children to communicate information and ideas using IT. In particular, communicating to a given audience (such as a younger friend) which needs to know about the enquiry, can foster skills of expression and can encourage discussion concerning the most appropriate language for that communication.

In the late 1990s, electronic communication is set to be one of the major growth areas in IT education (Donert, 1995). Many children are already becoming familiar with such techniques through home, friends and television. Good examples are:

1. The regular use of electronic mail by children's TV programmes.
2. The widely advertised development of the Internet to access remote sources of data.
3. The FAX, which is already acknowledged as an acceptable form of electronic communication.

Geography lends itself to these forms of communication, especially where it involves current events and long distances. For example, children at Key Stage 2 can communicate by FAX or e-mail with schools in contrasting regions in Britain or abroad. Organisations such as the Meteorological Office publish FAX numbers allowing access to a range of resources specifically for schools (Figure 3.7). Schools are thus able to download current weather maps, forecasts and satellite

IT strand	Detail	Possible examples in geography at Key Stage 2
Communicating and handling information	using IT to generate and communicate ideas in written, numerical visual or aural forms to a variety of audiences, to retrieve, analyse and amend information	a newsroom simulation including the wordprocessing of events following a disaster, communicate by a school link, faxing geographical information (maps and data) collected by children to other schools
Controlling	using IT to control external events	use a datalogger to collect and store weather information, use aerial photographs to plan developments in the local area
Modelling	exploring computer representations of ideas and of real and imaginary situations	use computer software which simulates the movement of nomadic tribes in the Sahel, or water flowing in a drainage basin
Monitoring	using IT to keep track of external events	use satellite images to investigate the passage of a storm use aerial photographs to look at land uses changes in the local area.

Figure 3.6 Information technology strands and possible geographical interpretations. Source: adapted from SCAA (1995).

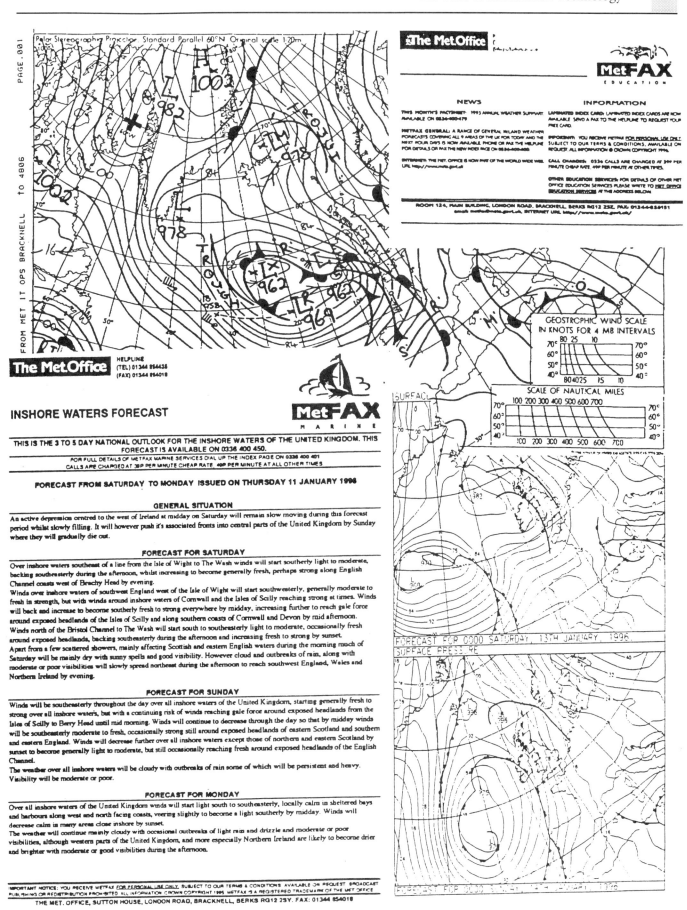

Figure 3.7 MetFAX – weather data by FAX.

images of Britain (and beyond), as well as fact sheets and other information. This, combined with an enquiry-based sequence of weather data collection as suggested by Bowden (1995), is found in many primary schools.

Electronic mail (e-mail) requires a simple piece of equipment (a modem) to link the computer to the normal telephone system. Written messages can then be sent from one computer to another anywhere in the world, all for the price of a local call. E-mail is widely used in industry, research, commerce, government and higher education. It is also becoming more regularly used in primary and secondary schools, with several readily accessible projects focused on schools. For example, links with schools in Australia, South Africa and the Netherlands may be established by obtaining e-mail addresses from the Internet (see Section 5 below). Schools are able to test and trial on-line Internet access through pilot projects such as *Project Connect*.

Control, Modelling and Monitoring

Other opportunities to develop IT in Key Stage 2 teaching include *control, modelling and monitoring*. *Modelling* software is used to recreate real and imaginary situations for children to investigate. They make use of simulations, adventure programs, spreadsheets and programming languages such as Logo. In this way children can explore geographical patterns, relationships and changes, such as those involved in the siting of a new power station. Measurement and *control* can involve children using a computer as a datalogger, with sensors to record and collect data which have been remotely sensed, as part of environmental *monitoring*. In this way, remote and hazardous environments can be investigated. Water pollution and weather conditions, such as temperature, light and humidity, can readily be monitored in a straightforward and user friendly way (Bowden, 1993).

The effects of IT on society are enormous. A practical example of this is the production and analysis of satellite imagery and aerial photographs. There are a large number of geographical uses that images from satellites such as Landsat have been put to (Chambers et al, 1989). These applications range from weather forecasting to monitoring global issues of environmental concern such as the ozone layer. Satellites enable detailed mapping of land use, soil and vegetation. They can identify icebergs and are used to map wave heights, wind patterns, river sediments and pollution. Virtually all aspects of geography have become measurable from space. More on this in Section 5.

Section 3: The Role of IT in the Geography National Curriculum

There are three key aims involved in using IT:

1. To develop children's IT skills and abilities.
2. To improve children's learning in geography.
3. To foster learning by the integration of IT skills and geography.

Some ways they might be developed in geography at Key Stage 2 are shown in Figure 3.8.

Key aims	Examples in geography
IT skills and abilities	The presentation and analysis of geographical data and information, including the manipulation of text and data, the storage and retrieval of information, communicating by transferring information using a FAX or modem
Improving children's learning in geography	Better access to information and knowledge, greater motivation using a database to explore large amounts of information which would not normally be possible, for example when using a CD-ROM to look at pictures and video to learn about geographical processes and features
Integrating IT and geography	Using satellite images of the Earth's surface and weather systems, the collection of weather information using a datalogger

Figure 3.8 Meeting key IT aims in geography.

Core Skills in IT

Attitudes to IT are changing (see Figure 3.9). The importance of enhancing children's learning through the use of computers is now more widely accepted. However, many teachers are concerned that they do not know or understand how computers work. They may feel intimidated by the technology or terminology, and as a result may not use IT. In fact, in order to teach geography using IT, very few basic skills are needed (see Figure 3.10). All of these are simple and easy to apply, with level 10 being the most important. It is important for teachers to:

1. Address classroom management issues thoroughly.
2. Be prepared to learn from experience.
3. Feel comfortable with a few basic IT skills (see Figure 3.10).
4. Be prepared to ask for help when they need it.

Figure 3.9 Some reasons teachers give for not using IT.

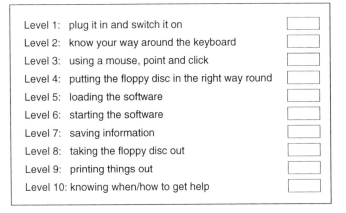

Figure 3.10 Some National Curriculum IT skills for teachers: how do you score?

Providing IT: Confidence, Competence and Preparation

Developing children's IT capabilities is mainly a question of confidence, together with a little IT competence and considerable preparation. This is especially the case if you are new to the materials, processes or ideas. Your pupils will probably have already developed a range of practical IT skills. They are likely to have had considerable experience in using computers at home and in Key Stage 1. Some will help you out in an emergency, as they will have used packages for wordprocessing, drawing, data analysis and presentation. Your main task is to relate children's IT work to Key Stage 2, so you will need to consider how the use of IT affects teaching style and children's learning.

There are three ways to approach IT. You are likely to be undertaking one of the following:

1. Introducing new IT skills.
2. Reinforcing existing IT skills.
3. Developing existing IT skills further and introducing new ones.

The objectives must be clear in terms of the knowledge, understanding and skills associated with geography and how the use and development of IT skills can support these objectives. The following sections provide guidance on this.

As you use and develop IT in your teaching, so your confidence with the technology will increase and your competence in management will improve. It is often simply the case of taking the plunge, then, as you use and perfect one IT application in your teaching scheme, so others become possible. In-service training may become a high priority in order to help you achieve this. Building on your strengths and recognising your weaknesses are often the keys to progress.

Managing IT

You will need to use a variety of classroom management strategies to cope with IT in your own school circumstances. Several teaching styles associated with computers have been identified (see Figure 3.11). Each is valid and useful in certain circumstances. In most situations, interaction between pupils and computer is more productive than tasks which require a more passive approach.

So, in order to be successful in using IT in the classroom, you will need to achieve three things:

1. Implement IT in your lessons.
2. Manage IT so that pupil learning is efficient and effective.
3. Evaluate the ways you have used IT and consider how to improve them.

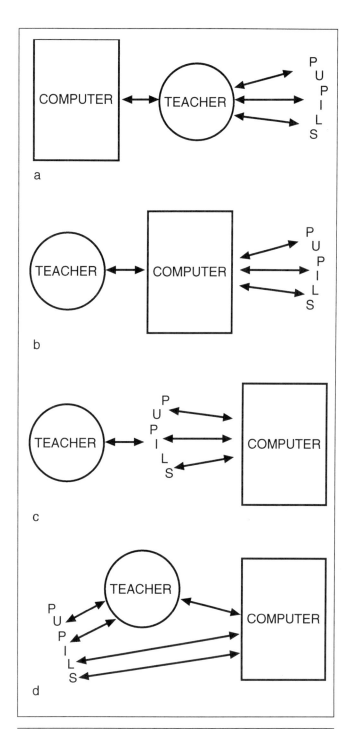

a

b

c

d

Figure 3.11 Four styles of using computers to teach geography.
Source: (MESU), NCET (1988).

Section 4: Planning for IT

Teachers will need to allocate time to ensure that every child develops IT capability. This time is required both for teaching IT skills, knowledge and understanding and for practising and consolidating them (SCAA, 1995).

It is helpful to classify IT activities in terms of focus:

1. Mainly IT development alone.
2. IT development as well as the skills, knowledge and understanding in geography.
3. The skills, knowledge and understanding of geography through the use of IT.

Planning for IT in subjects like geography will involve a number of important steps (Figure 3.12). You will need to decide whether you want to plan geography and IT separately or together. The IT you use needs to be appropriate for children, for you, for the classroom, for the school and for the whole curriculum. This means there are pressures on you to provide relevant and useful IT opportunities.

But What Are You Aiming For?

Pupils should be taught to extend the range of IT tools that they use for communication, investigation and control; become discerning in their use of IT; select information sources and media for their suitability for purpose; and assess the value of IT in their working practices.

(At Key Stage 2), *Pupils should be given opportunities to:*

1a   *use IT to explore and solve problems in the context of work across a variety of subjects;*
1b   *use IT to further their understanding of information that they have retrieved and processed;*
1c   *discuss their experiences of using IT and assess its value in their working practices;*
1d   *investigate parallels with the use of IT in the wider World, consider the effects of such uses, and compare them with other methods.*
(DFE, 1995b)

This means you need to plan your IT opportunities to cover geographical knowledge, skills and understanding through themes and places in your scheme of work. Look at different areas of the key stage where IT might be appropriate, select feasible activities and do not try to be over ambitious.

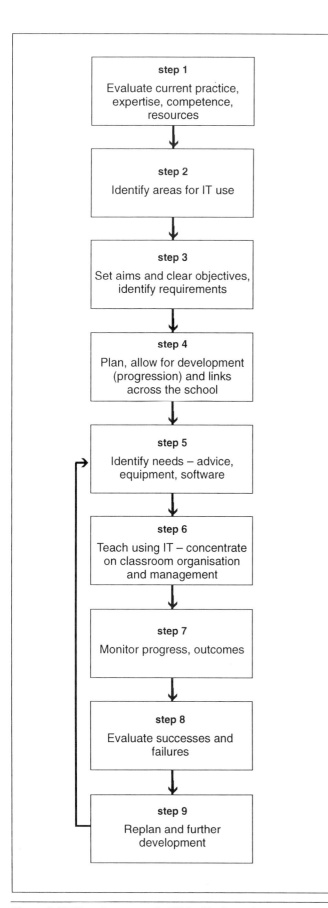

Figure 3.12 Planning process in IT for Key Stage 2.

Consider the possible alternatives and how existing IT resources might be tied into the geographical work. Lists of suitable IT applications are readily available from Geographical Association publications (Eades and Weldon, 1995) and NCET, whereas many IT ideas and activities have been provided by the GA in publications such as *Primary Geographer*, for example by Russell (1995).

Planning for Progression

It is necessary to structure teaching styles and learning activities to build upon experience already gained by pupils. It is important to achieve this without too much repetition. Progression needs to be considered in three main areas:

1. Cognitive development of the pupil.
2. The logical sequence of the subject matter.
3. The progression of the resources involved, in this case IT and geography materials.

In achieving this, the experiences of IT need to be introduced, consolidated and extended across the curriculum. Clear progression needs to be identified (see Figure 3.13). This should include the level of pupils' confidence in using IT and the degree of independence achieved. You should also take account of past learning in key stage 1 and what is taking place in other subjects. Both of these imply a whole school approach to IT. Once you have drawn up your plan, an initial evaluation will help you assess its potential effectiveness. A number of relevant questions can be asked (see Figure 3.14).

Resourcing IT

In some cases IT remains the most under used and redundant school resource. Equipment and software may have been obtained but not widely integrated into teaching schemes. You may be surprised to find out precisely what resources are held by the school.

Before developing a new IT resource you will need to find out the following:

1. Where are the resources located?
2. How is it used, and who is it used by?
3. What else can it be used for?
4. How can you gain access to the resource?
5. What do you need to do in order to use the resource?
6. Who might be able to assist you in developing the resource?

IT for a weather teaching scheme

Drawing weather, using a **painting software** to draw a picture about the weather

Making up weather symbols, further developing the use of a **painting software** drawing more precise objects

Using newspaper or **wordprocessing** software to write a story about the weather

Using **graphing software** to present simple information collected about the weather

Use of **CD-ROM database** (encyclopaedia to look up different types of weather, collect text and pictures)

Use **datalogger** to collect detailed weather data (such as temperature, pressure, wind speed, direction) over a longer period of time

Use of **database** or **spreadsheet** software to investigate data obtained from the datalogger

Use satellite imagery of weather, use video clips to **explain how IT is used** to collect the information

Use of **Metfax** to receive faxed weather maps and satellite images from the Met Office, **use of IT in communicating information**

Use of **the Internet** to receive weather information, satellite images and maps, **use of IT in communicating information** in a more interactive way, e-mail class weather reports to linked schools

Figure 3.13 Possible IT progression for a weather teaching scheme at Key Stage 2.

Is IT integrated into the curriculum/scheme of work?

1. Is the IT balanced?
         relevant?

2. Does the IT allow for differentiation?
                      progression?
                      continuity?

3. Has appropriate IT been used for the pupils
                      the geographical themes?
                      the places?

4. Has a suitable methodology (enquiry) been encouraged?

5. Has IT helped teaching and learning?

6. Has the IT been applied equally across abilities?
                      the needs of the pupils?

Figure 3.14 Key questions in planning for IT.

Remember when considering the use of an IT resource for the first time, that there will also be questions of:

1. Compatibility (will it work on your computer?).
2. Standardisation (can it be used by all pupils?).
3. Continuity (have they done it before?).
4. Transferability (is it building on existing skills or developing new ones?).
5. Development (does it enhance existing work?).
6. Usefulness (can it be done better in another way?).
7. Price (is it too expensive for its use?).
8. Upgrades (will I need to improve it in the near future and will that be expensive?).

Section 5: New IT Developments

Several new IT applications deserve a mention at this point. Developments in computer technology and communications are increasing at a rapid rate. Three of the most striking recent developments are elaborated below: the Internet, CD-ROMs and satellite remote sensing. Of these, it is the first two which are set to have the greatest impact on children's learning in geography, partly because of their wide application, their steadily falling hardware prices and their ease of access.

The Internet and World Wide Web

Communication by e-mail and FAX enables pupils at different schools to establish benefical links easily. They can exchange information about the schools and surrounding areas. Even greater interaction is allowed through World Wide Web (WWW) on the Internet, where pictures, sounds, video clips and text can be left on a *home page* for other schools to access, at the price of a local telephone call. Schools are increasingly producing their own home pages (see Figure 3.15), offering a range of information about themselves and the areas in which they are located. Many commercial and voluntary organisations have established or make use of WWW sites which can be accessed by anyone on the Internet. Examples of relevance to school geography include environmental bodies (eg Friends of the Earth), government agencies, companies, educational organisations, schools, universities and individuals.

Frithwood Primary School Home Page

Frithwood Primary School, Carew Road, Northwood, Middlesex, HA6 3NJ, England. Tel: 01923 825548
These pages were produced by the headteacher, staff, pupils and governors and last updated on 17 September 1995.

Photos of School/ Pupil's work/ Art Week/ Helicopter/ Music/ Quiet Area/ Ofsted/ Web Links/ I.T.

The School

☐ Frithwood School is a County Primary Co-Educational Day School under the jurisdiction of the London Borough of Hillingdon. The school took its first intake of Infant and Junior children of both sexes in September 1978 and the Nursery class opened a month later. There are 40 pupils in the Nursery, 100 in the Infant department and 110 in the Junior department.

Five photographs of the school are included in this gallery. Each is thumbnail size for speed of loading but can be viewed full size by clicking on the photograph in the gallery.

Here are 2 additional sources of information on the school (both Microsoft Word 6 documents).
Click here to download information from the prospectus (frithinf.doc 12.8k).
Click here to download information from the Annual Parents Report (gov-apm.doc 67k).

Children's Work and Link Magazine

The Frithwood School Association produces a magazine of children's work; stories, poems, drawings and jokes for parents each term called the Link Magazine. Click here to see children's work and the Link Magazine.

Helicopters!!

Last year we had a visit from a Helicopter. It flew round the school and landed on the playing field.

Figure 3.15 An Internet 'home page'.

CD-ROMs

CD-ROMs were introduced on page 45. They allow pupils to explore a large amount of information in their own way and by their own route. The information on a CD-ROM can be provided in the form of text, pictures, video clips, animation and sound. The combination of these in a single package is known as multimedia. The best CD-ROMS have the ability to test the pupils' learning and the acquisition of skills, as well as recording the results. In this way enquiry-based learning is encouraged and assessment is managed through the technology.

The CD-ROM allows pupils to access many places in the World which are not available otherwise. The number of CD-ROMs suitable for Key Stage 2 is rapidly growing and the quality and usefulness are improving. The same CD-ROMs can now be used on different types of computer (platforms), thus enhancing their usefulness, flexibility and practicality. The regular use of CD-ROMs will become commonplace in the classrooms of the future. Already encyclopaedias, newspapers, atlases and databases are widely used in local libraries and in secondary schools. There are also many more geography specific CD-ROMs on the way, as the subject readily lends itself to multimedia developments.

Satellite Remote Sensing

Remote sensing by satellites also requires a special mention here. Several useful packs have already been developed. Some are only for in-service training purposes, though most are for use in the classroom. They normally consist of teachers' notes, sets of classroom resources (satellite images and posters) and photocopiable worksheets. They are usually visually stunning, and are supplemented by a variety of very useful activities and exercises. To support these, a valuable purchase would be a set of magnifying glasses. The two main types of satellite image most suitable for Key Stage 2 are weather satellite images, showing cloudy and clear areas. These will be familiar to pupils on television weather forecasts.

The second type of image shows differences in ground cover (eg land use, sea temperatures). These often make use of false colour to reveal differences in temperature and land use which cannot be seen with normal light. Understandably, children at Key Stage 2 can find false colour somewhat confusing. Simple activites matching specific colours and land uses can help. The recent Geographical Association publication on remote sensing (Barnett et al, 1995) is invaluable. Satellite images can be obtained on floppy disc or direct from the Internet.

IT Glossary

CD-ROM (Compact Disc – Read Only Memory) is a means of storing large amounts of digital data. It enables the equivalent of 300 reference books or 2000 high quality images to be stored. It can contain text, graphics, animation and sound – hence the term multimedia is often used. Some are specifically geography eg *Map Skills* (Pebbleshore), others have a significant geographical content (*CD Atlas*), and some are general references and have much wider use eg encyclopaedias and newspapers.

Concept keyboard, or overlay keyboard is a touch sensitive device which can be incorporated with a computer.

Data handling software allows the presentation of fieldwork data in suitable forms (eg graphs and sometimes maps) and enables calculations to be carried out.

Database software enables relationships to be explored quickly and easily, information can be sorted and analysed and presented efficiently and effectively, eg *Key*

Datalogger is usually a small piece of equipment with sensors which measures and stores information.

Desktop publishing software allows text, diagrams, pictures, data and graphs to be presented together in a coherent, single document.

Drill and practice software, allows exercises or revision to be undertaken.

Electronic mail (e-mail) allows text communication from one computer via a telephone link, or modem, to other computers in other parts of the world.

FAX machine transmits information read from sheets of paper (text, maps and pictures) via a telephone line to another machine elsewhere in the world.

Graphics software packages enable drawings to be made on computer and pictures to be altered. Modelling packages and simulations allow students to investigate situations, questioning events and predicting outcomes.

Internet is a system of communicating with computers and computer networks world-wide, usually via a modem and telephone link. It requires specific software to access it, but costs are relatively cheap. Vast amounts of geographical information are available and can be taken from the Internet onto your computer.

Modem is a piece of equipment which attaches to a computer and enables access to the Internet via a telephone connection.

*Multimedia software/*CD-ROM provides information in a variety of forms, usually text and pictures, but more often also in the form of animation, video clips and sound.

Newsroom simulation software is wordprocessing or desktop publishing software which allows the production of newspaper-like layout.

Scanner is a piece of equipment which enables pictures and text to be transformed from paper format into the computer's digital format.

Simulation software mimics a real world situation, which would either be impossible to see or difficult to understand. (eg the structure of the Earth or changes in the population of an area).

Spreadsheet software (for example *Excel*) enables data to be calculated, allows modelling to take place – creating 'what if' scenarios. It enables the exploration of concepts and ideas which would not be possible otherwise or would be too time consuming.

Wordprocessing software allows text to entered, edited and stored. The style and presentation can be altered.

A checklist to ensure that geography is in your topic

Topic Title:

Other contributing subjects and time allowance:

1.

2.

3.

Geography: Knowledge

Is the distribution of features and places considered?

Are similarities and differences emphasised?

Are several localities at different scales utilised?

Is the interaction between people and places featured?

Are physical and human features emphasised?

Are connections and routes between places noted?

Geography: Skills

Are maps used?

Are atlases used?

Are globes used?

Are fieldwork and practical work used?

Are aerial or satellite photographs used?

Is the topic enquiry-based?

Are issues discussed?

Geography: Values

Is the interdependence of localities and countries mentioned?

Is the responsibility of human beings for their environment stressed?

Is an attempt made to empathise with other cultures and lifestyles?

Are other points of view analysed?

Is there a respect for evidence and an attempt to identify bias and prejudice?

Is action to care for the environment encouraged?

Place	Feature	Name	Topic in which covered	Known? (by children)
United Kingdom	Mountains & uplands	Grampian Mountains Pennines Lake District Cambrian		
	Rivers	Trent Severn Thames		
	Seas	Irish Sea English Channel		
	Countries	Scotland Northern Ireland England Wales		
	Capitals and towns	Edinburgh Belfast Cardiff London		
Europe	Mountains & uplands	Alps		
	Rivers	Rhine		
	Seas	North Sea Mediterranean Sea		
	Countries	Republic of Ireland United Kingdom Germany France Italy Spain		
	Capitals and towns	Dublin London Berlin Paris Madrid Rome		

/continued

THIS PAGE MAY BE PHOTOCOPIED FOR USE IN SCHOOL

Place	Feature	Name	Topic in which covered	Known? (by children)
World	Mountains & uplands	Rocky Mountains Himalayas Andes		
	Rivers	Mississippi Nile Amazon		
	Seas & oceans	Arctic Atlantic Pacific Indian		
	Pole	North South		
	Tropics	Cancer Capricorn Equator		
	Meridian	Prime		
	Desert	Sahara		
	Canals	Suez Panama		
	Continents	North America Europe Asia Africa South America Oceania Antarctica		
	Countries	Canada Russian Federation USA China India Brazil Indonesia Australia		
	Capitals & towns	Paris New York Cairo Bombay Sydney Buenos Aires		

THIS PAGE MAY BE PHOTOCOPIED FOR USE IN SCHOOL

A planning and audit matrix for cross curricular themes and geography

Geography topic	Cross curricular link or context				
	Economic & industrial under-standing	Health education	Careers education	Environ-mental education	Citizenship
Make and use maps Use atlas Use globe Use aerial photographs Carry out fieldwork					
School locality					
Contrasting UK locality African, Asian, S. or C. American (including Caribbean) locality					
Physical features Human features Interrelationship of features					
Changes in localities Localities in broader context Localities' links with other places Similarities and differences in localities					
Topical examples: United Kingdom context Topical examples: European Union context					
River systems River processes and features					
Weather: microclimate Weather: seasons Weather: worldwide					
Settlement: hierarchy Settlement: function Settlement: location Settlement: land use Settlement: land use issue Settlement: change					
Environmental change: human impact Environmental change: management					

THIS PAGE MAY BE PHOTOCOPIED FOR USE IN SCHOOL

You can claim to be good if you tick the following boxes:

I integrate skills, themes and places ❑

I include the study of a range of types of real places across the world ❑

I ensure progression across the key stages ❑

I provide a range of assessment opportunities that are integral to the learning process ❑

I stress the contribution of geography to the key skills including IT ❑

I ensure that the total experience is geographically broad, balanced and relevant ❑

I give experiences outside the classroom ❑

I use maps of real places and develop concepts of scale ❑

I look for patterns in distribution ❑

I look for relationships between people and places ❑

I describe the world in different ways ❑

I use specialist vocabulary, maps, diagrams and models ❑

I use children's own experiences and knowledge ❑

I give access to a wide range of up to date visual materials (pictures, maps, diagrams, and data) ❑

I use the enquiry process through questioning ❑

You should start to worry if you tick the following boxes:

Mapwork is taught in isolation as a separate topic ❑

Pupils do compass work without seeing a compass ❑

My work rigidly follows a published scheme ❑

There is little mention of geography in my curriculum plans ❑

Geography is not based on real people and places ❑

There are not sufficient materials ❑

Pupils are doing 'all about' projects on countries, involving much copying ❑

I am unclear about the uniqueness of geography ❑

How do I rate on differentiation?
Ten questions to ask yourself

		Scoring 1 = low 5 = high	Comments on scoring	Action/targets
1	Do I organise my teaching group to enable differentiation?			
2	Do I manage the classroom space to aid differentiation?			
3	Have I discussed with colleagues specific ways of teacher intervention which may be used to achieve differentiation?			
4	Have I established useful links with support teachers in sharing and identifying learning needs?			
5	How much importance do I attach to links between assessment and future learning in geography?			
6	Do I involve children in measuring their success in geography by sharing learning objectives with them?			
7	Does my planning of learning objectives and activities in geography identify an essential core, reinforcement and extension work?			
8	Are geographical materials prepared to allow for differentiation?			
9	Do I vary my teaching style to support differentiation?			
10	Where does planning for differentiation lie in the priorities of the School Development Plan?			

Source: Piggott B (1995) Differentiation in geography. *Primary Geographer, 21*

Planning for information technology in geography at Key Stage 2

Year	Use of IT in geography	Topic	IT skills	Geography skills	Resources needed
3					
4					
5					
6					

Location

Time of Year

Year group

Theme

Observation and collection of information	talk	☐	see	☐
	question	☐	feel	☐
	discuss	☐	smell	☐
	follow instructions	☐	other	☐
	listen	☐		

Recording of information	write	☐	photograph	☐
	draw	☐	video	☐
	sketch	☐	audio	☐
	measure	☐	other	☐

Analysis and conclusion	tabulate	☐	compare	☐
	map	☐	contrast	☐
	graph	☐	identify	☐
			other	☐

Type of presentation of information (output)	report	☐	as an individual	☐
	poster	☐	in a group	☐
	project	☐	to the public	☐
	other	☐	to the class	☐
			to the school	☐
			other	☐

Chambers and Donert: Teaching Geography at Key Stage 2

Chris Kington Publishi

IT activity/resource	Geographical skills			Geographical theme				Locality		
	maps	photos	others	rivers	weather	settlement	environment	school	contrasting locality 1	contrasting locality 2

References and Bibliography

Bailey P. and Binns J.A. (eds) (1987) *A Case for Geography.* Sheffield, The Geographical Association

Barnett M., Kent A. and Milton M. (1995) *Images of the Earth: a Teacher's Guide to Remote Sensing in Geography at Key Stage 2.* Sheffield, The Geographical Association

Bennetts T. (1995) 'Continuity and progression'. *Primary Geographer* 21, pp 44-46

Bland K., Chambers W., Donert K. and Thomas A.D. (1996) 'Fieldwork in geography' in Bailey P. (ed) *Handbook for Geography Teachers.* Sheffield, The Geographical Association

Blyth A. and Krause J. (1995) *Primary Geography: a Developmental Approach.* London, Hodder and Stoughton

Booth R., Chambers W.J. and Thomas A.D. (1993) *Reaching Out.* London, Living Earth/ICI

Bowden D. (1991) 'IT: off the shelf or self help?'. *Primary Geographer* 6, pp 11-12

Bowden D. (1992) 'Geography software: the state of the art'. *Primary Geographer* 11, pp 18-19

Bowden D. (1993) 'Datalogging – an introduction' *Primary Geographer* 12, p 20

Bowden D. (1995) 'Bringing IT down to earth'. *Primary Geographer* 20, p 25

Bowles R. (1993) *Resources for Key Stage 1, 2 and 3.* Sheffield, The Geographical Association

Brough E. (1983) 'Geography through art' in Huckle J. (ed) *Geographical Education: Reflection and Action.* Oxford, Oxford University Press

Butt G., Lambert D. and Telfer S. (1995) *Assessment Works.* Sheffield, The Geographical Association

Catling S. (1990) 'Resourcing mapwork'. *Primary Geographer* 5, p 14

Catling S. (1995) 'Choosing and using places'. *Primary Geographer* 21, pp 20-23

Chambers W. (1992) 'Some approaches to teaching distant locations' in de Villiers M., *Primary Geography Matters: Change in the Geography Curriculum.* Sheffield, The Geographical Association

Chambers W. (1995) *Awareness in Action: Environmental Education in the Primary Curriculum.* Sheffield, The Geographical Association

Chambers W. and Donert K. (1995) *Nelson Atlas.* Walton-on-Thames, Nelson

Chambers W., Nelder G., Paterson K. and Wareing H. (1989) 'Viewing the earth from space'. *Primary Geographer* 1, pp 7-10

Committee of Enquiry into the Education of Handicapped Children and Young People (1978) *Special Educational Needs.* London, HMSO

Council for Environmental Education (1994) *English and Environmental Education.* Reading, CEE

Council for Environmental Education (1994) *Environmental Education and Geography.* Reading, CEE

Curriculum Council for Wales (1991) *Geography in the National Curriculum: Non-Statutory Guidance for Teachers.* Cardiff, Welsh Office

Curriculum Council for Wales (1992) *INSET Activities for National Curriculum Geography.* Cardiff, Curriculum Council for Wales

Daugherty R. (ed) (1989) *Geography in the National Curriculum.* Sheffield, The Geographical Association

Davidson J. and Krause J. (eds.) (1991) *Geography, IT and the National Curriculum.* Sheffield, Geographical Association

Davidson J. and Rudd M. (eds.) (1993) *IT and Geography at Key Stages 3 and 4.* Sheffield, Geographical Association

Dearing R. (1994) *The National Curriculum and its Assessment.* London, Schools Curriculum Assessment Authority

Dearing R. (1993) *The National Curriculum and its Assessment: Final Report.* London, Schools Curriculum Assessment Authority

Department of Education and Science (1986) *Geography from 5 to 16.* London, HMSO

Department for Education (1995a) *Geography in the National Curriculum.* London, HMSO

Department for Education (1995b) *Information Technology in the National Curriculum.* London, HMSO

Department for Education (1995c) *Key Stages 1 and 2 of the National Curriculum.* London, HMSO

Dilkes J. L. and Nicholls A. (1988) *Low Attainers and the Teaching of Geography.* Sheffield, The Geographical Association and The National Association for Remedial Education

Donert K. (1995) 'Along the superhighway and into the classroom'. *OLS News* 63, pp 11-12

Eades K. and Weldon M. (1995) 'IT and geography: the Lincolnshire solution'. *Primary Geographer* 20, p 30

Foley M. and Janikoun J. (1992) *The Really Practical Guide to Primary Geography.* Cheltenham, Stanley Thornes

Geography and IT Support Project (1995) *Primary Geography: a Pupil's Entitlement to IT.* Sheffield, NCET and Geographical Association

Harwood D. (1992) 'Learning about location, ideas for spreadsheets in primary geography'. *Primary Geographer* 10, pp 12-13

Her Majesty's Inspectorate (1989) *The Teaching and Learning of History and Geography in the Primary School.* London, HMSO

Hindson J. (1989) 'Managing resources', in Wiegand P. *Managing the Geography Department.* Sheffield, The Geographical Association

Hughes J. (1992) 'The cost of resourcing the geography curriculum'. *Primary Geographer* 11, p 9

Hughes J. and Marsden W. (1994) 'Resourcing primary geography: bringing the world into the classroom', in Marsden W. and Hughes J. (eds) *Primary School Geography*. London, David Fulton

John M. (1995) 'Models for a mixed economy'. *Times Educational Supplement Computers Update*, March 24 1995, p 36

Kent A. and Philips A. (1994) 'Geography through information technology: supporting geographical enquiry,' in Marsden W. and Hughes J. (eds) *Primary School Geography*. London, David Fulton

Lawson K. and Schiavone T. (1995) 'Out with the old, in with the new?' *Primary Geographer* 21, pp 24-26

Lewis E. and Watts S. (1995) 'A world of words – primary geography and language development'. *Primary Geographer* 21, pp 33-35

MacColl P. (1984) In Fien J. (ed) *The Geography Teacher's Guide to the Classroom*. London, Macmillan

May S. and Cook J. (1993a) 'Fieldwork in action – an enquiry approach', in de Villiers M. (ed) *Primary Geography Matters: Children's Worlds*. Sheffield, The Geographical Association

May S. and Cook J. (1993b) *Fieldwork in action: an enquiry approach*. Sheffield, The Geographical Association

MESU (1988) *Learning Geography with Computers*. Coventry, MESU

Mills D. (1988) 'Talking, reading, writing and geographical work' in Mills D. (ed) *Geographical Work in Primary and Middle Schools*. Sheffield, The Geographical Association

Morgan W. (1991) *A National Curriculum Guide (for Teachers) to Geographical Work in Primary and Middle Schools*. Sheffield, The Geographical Association.

Morgan W. (1992) *Focus on Castries St. Lucia*. Sheffield, The Geographical Association

Morgan W. (1993) *Geography in a Nutshell*. Sheffield, The Geographical Association

Morgan W. (1995a) *Plans for Primary Geography*. Sheffield, The Geographical Association

Morgan W. (1995b) 'Over the horizon: teaching about distant places'. *Primary Geographer* 21, pp 27-29

National Curriculum Council (1989) *A Curriculum for All*. York, NCC

National Curriculum Council (1990a) *Careers Education*. York, NCC

National Curriculum Council (1990b) *Economic and Industrial Understanding*. York, NCC

National Curriculum Council (1990c) *Environmental Education*. York, NCC

National Curriculum Council (1990d) *Health Education*. York, NCC

National Curriculum Council (1991a) *Citizenship*. York, NCC

National Curriculum Council (1991b) *Geography Non-Statutory Guidance*. York, NCC

National Curriculum Council (1993a) *An Introduction to Teaching Geography at Key Stages 1 and 2*. York, NCC

National Curriculum Council (1993b) *Teaching Geography at Key Stages 1 and 2: an INSET Guide*. York, NCC

NCET (1988) *Learning Geography with Computers Pack*. Coventry, NCET

NCET (1995) *Approaches to IT Capability: Key Stages 1 and 2*. Coventry, NCET

Office for Standards in Education (1993) *Geography: Key Stages 1, 2 and 3: First Year, 1991-92*. London, HMSO

Office for Standards in Education (1995) *Geography: a Review of Inspection Findings 1993/94*. London, HMSO

Palmer J. (1994) *Geography in the Early Years*. London, Routledge

Piggott B. (1993) 'Differentiation in geography'. *Primary Geographer* 15, pp 15-17

Piggott B. (1995) 'Differentiation in geography'. *Primary Geographer* 21, pp 30-32

Ranger G. (1995) 'A slimmer, trimmer geography – the rationale for curriculum change'. *Primary Geographer* 21 pp 4-6 and pp 5-7

Rawling E. (1986) 'Approaches to teaching and learning', in Boardman D. (ed) *Handbook for Geography Teachers*. Sheffield, The Geographical Association

Rawling E. (1991) 'Spirit of enquiry falls off the map' *Times Educational Supplement*, 25 January

Rawling E. (1992) *Programmes of Study: Try This Approach*. Sheffield, The Geographical Association

Russell K. (1995) 'IT and geography in the revised curriculum'. *Primary Geographer* 21, pp 39-41

Schools Curriculum Assessment Authority (1995) *Key Stages 1 and 2: Information Technology – the New Requirements*. London, Schools Curriculum Assessment Authority

School Curriculum and Assessment Authority (1995) *Planning the Curriculum at Key Stages 1 and 2*. London, Schools Curriculum Assessment Authority

Sebba J. (1991) *Planning for Geography for Pupils with Learning Difficulties*. Sheffield, The Geographical Association

Sebba J. (1995) *Geography for All*. London, David Fulton

Serf J. (1988) 'The way forward – where do we go from here? The opinions of one geography teacher' in Dilkes J. L. and Nicholls A. (eds) *Low Attainers and the Teaching of Geography*. Sheffield, The Geographical Association and The National Association for Remedial Education

Smith S. (1988) 'Geography for children with special educational needs' in Mills D. (ed) *Geographical Work in Primary and Middle Schools*. Sheffield, The Geographical Association

Smith S. and Richardson P. (1995) 'Access for all: special educational needs'. *Primary Geographer* 21, pp. 36-38

Storm M. (1989) 'The five basic questions for primary geography'. *Primary Geographer* 2, p 4

Tidy Britain Group (1993) *Education for Citizenship.* Wigan, TBG

Trend R.D. (ed) (1995) *Geography and Science: Forging Links at Key Stage 3.* Sheffield, The Geographical Association

Warnock M. (1978) *Special Educational Needs.* London, HMSO

Wiegand P. (1993) *Children and Primary Geography.* London, Cassell

Yeomans D. and Wiegand P. (1993) *Report on the Evaluation of the Remote Sensing Element of the Welsh Office Satellites in Schools Initiative.* Coventry, NCET

Index